CHANGING QUALITIES OF CHINESE LIFE

By the same author

GOVERNMENT AND REVOLUTION IN VIETNAM
THE PEACETIME STRATEGY OF THE CHINESE
  PEOPLE'S REPUBLIC

Urbanization in Hong Kong — the old life cornered by the new
(by courtesy of the Hong Kong Government).

CHANGING QUALITIES OF CHINESE LIFE

Dennis Duncanson

First published 1982 by
THE MACMILLAN PRESS LTD
London and Basingstoke
Companies and representatives
throughout the world

ISBN 0 333 30682 1

Printed in Hong Kong

Contents

List of Plates

1 Perceptions of Chinese Life

'... at thirty, one's attitude is self-confident ... at sixty, one is more discriminating'

(Analects of Confucius)

The reader will not find a documented treatise here. The book is, without apology, personal – eclectic, discursive, impressionistic. There exist plenty of methodical treatises on topics discussed in it – on the rural industries of China, for example, or on recondite and controversial subjects such as industrial relations in Hong Kong or the Chinese share of the retail trade in Indonesia. One recent treatise sounds close to my theme – *Value Change in Chinese Society*,[1] by a team of American professors; I have benefited from some of the facts it brings to light, but it only deals with small parts of my chosen field. An insight both deeper and broader is to be had from *The China Difference*[2] by another team of American professors (edited by Ross Terrill), but its focus is the mainland at the present time and the ways in which life differs there from life in America. I know of no comparative overview of the quality of Chinese life as it has been lived, during the last few decades, under the variety of political, economic and social regimes that have imposed themselves on different communities of the Chinese people. My attempt at an overview brings together matter usually deemed proper for separate genres; it can explore none of them thoroughly and comes to few conclusions – it is one man's view.

The text began as a series of talks commissioned by the British Broadcasting Corporation after I had paid a return visit, in 1979, to countries in the Far East in which, for twenty and more of the middle years of my life, I earned my living constantly surrounded by Chinese faces. The tour I made, with my wife, was not a sentimental journey. I admire most things Chinese and prize the privilege of long association with that people; but it is hard to feel sentimentally towards a people whose own ethics spurn sentimentality and who make great show, at every juncture, of the didactic values by which they judge even questions of taste and art. My purpose was more practical and detached: I went in search of glimpses (one could not expect more) of the quality of life of Chinese people today – of Chinese people inside the People's Republic and in Taiwan, and also outside China, in what are called the Overseas Chinese communities of Hong Kong and Macau, of Singapore and Malaysia, Indonesia and Thailand.

My object was to make comparisons in both space and time. The comparison in time was to be the measure of how life has changed for different Chinese communities during the last three and a half decades – during the time that has elapsed since, scarcely out of uniform after a wartime apprenticeship as administrator and magistrate in ancient but rugged and backward Ethiopia, I first landed in a lush and sophisticated Malaya where, though my functions might carry the same titles as in Africa, all else was going to be utterly different. A few months after that first landing, but still two years before China was liberated by Mao Tsê-tung's Red Army, my employers, the colonial government of Malaya, sent me thither to learn to read Chinese and speak the Cantonese dialect, on pain of the sack if I did not satisfy a Hong Kong board of examiners every six months as to my progress. At the same time as I absorbed the language, I was supposed to soak myself in the Chinese way of life; the regulations for probationers left to chance the extent to which this second injunction was accomplished. What the adventure in travel and study entailed for members of my service was recorded at the time, with commendable sensitivity, by a colleague whom our employers dispatched to a different province of South China from mine but who, like me, wandered further afield than he was instructed to.[3]

Mao's Liberation of China was delayed by the god of people's war until my colleague and I had completed our probationary studies satisfactorily. I returned to the university to upgrade my Cantonese into Mandarin and to relate my practical impressions of the Chinese way of life to the political and cultural history of state and nation as they are recorded in the huge collections of Chinese literature. At the opposite end of the spectrum of personal experience – opposite to academe – I was posted next to the Singapore Government during the years of its transition to self-rule – the years when Professor Parkinson of the University of Malaya was working out his universal 'laws' of management and administration from observation of Europeans like me at work in harness with a rising generation of Overseas Chinese colleagues. I also took part in organizing the resistance to Mao's extension of Liberation to Malaya – again through the instrument of people's war – thereby meriting the status of *persona non grata* with the People's Government and the refusal in 1960 of a visa even to pass through China en route for the Trans-Siberian railway. By that time I had been appointed a civil servant in Hong Kong. After that, I did not improve my image in the eyes of the Chinese Communist Party by becoming an adviser to the much-reviled Ngo Dinh Diem in Vietnam during *his* resistance to people's war, and my return to the People's Republic in 1979 was at last made possible, less by any public change of heart on my part or of policy in Peking, than by the realization among Mao's successors of the potential of tourism as an earner of foreign exchange and of the unwisdom of picking and choosing between tourists – a realization, I hasten to add, that was reflected no less in the outstanding competence and good taste with which the tour was conducted. My journey to the Far East at large was planned in such a way as to enable me to move direct in space and directly in time, without intervening distractions, from Chinese communities under communist rule to Chinese communities outside it; that plan would enable me, I thought, to make a comparison in space.

Is there merit in perceptions of the quality of other people's life made up of these components – of former cohabitation (if I may so use that word), of years of study from a distance, and of recent flying visits? The reader must judge the special results after reading the book, but there are general objections that are liable to be raised in some quarters. First of all, there is the objection that 'the untrained observer' gains no true insight. Certainly, it is easy to misinterpret what you see:

nearly everywhere the urbanized Overseas Chinese are used
to indoor lavatories and main drains, whereas the Chinese at
home, even townspeople, still have lieux and manual disposal;
the difference looks like one of economic prosperity, but in
truth it owes more to the fact that China is predominantly
agricultural and needs huge quantities of untreated natural
manure, whereas the Overseas Chinese live far away from
food-growing. However, that is not what critics mean; their
objections are more profound. Working in a university, in
these days when the polymath is in bad odour, I frequently
hear criticisms voiced against other people for being 'untrained', but have noticed, as one decade melts into another,
that fashions in the conventional wisdom on what 'training' fits
the case and on what you are allowed to say you 'know' about
other people's ways of life undergo change after change.

Long ago, we only had occasional travellers' tales about the
Far East, interspersed with the plausible fictions of mounte-
banks. The Victorians improved on their predecessors'
accounts of China through the memoirs of soldiers, diplomats
or administrators, which sometimes resembled, as it happens,
the memoirs about unfamiliar provinces it had for centuries
been the duty of Chinese mandarins to compose *en poste* and
for their sons to publish after their death. In this century,
observation of the exotic all over the world has become subject
to the discipline of social science method, but even the
'method' has changed with fashion. For example, the social
anthropologists who came in with the First World War and
spent a year or two in one Asian village, recording as much as
they could about the people's lives in every respect possible,[4]
had to give way after the Second World War to a generation
exemplified by the contributors to *Value Change in Chinese
Society*, who have spent a shorter time investigating narrower
fields of social life in search of common ground with Africa or
South America. Fortunately, the same years gave rise also in
the China field to studies quite impervious to hypotheses
dictated from other continents – studies like the late Maurice
Freedman's on the 'lineages' of South China, which keep
cropping up in later chapters of this book. Like the anthropologists, the learned 'epistemologists' of politics compart-
mentalized their science too: formerly concerned primarily
to analyse the art of government and the motives of rulers,

they shifted ground to minimize the part played in political life by human will and to concentrate on the unconscious, the aberrant, and the popular – an equivalent 'method' to history-without-kings-and-battles. Computerized statistics have tended to supersede personal judgement, purporting to convert subjective data into objective analyses; the observer who wants to be reckoned 'trained' has continually to retool himself, keeping abreast not so much of advances in a positive science as of vogues in theory.

Persistent tension arose in the last years of the British Colonial Service between generalist administrators, who knew all about their colony but nothing about anywhere else, and visiting specialists from the changing schools of applied social science who knew something about everywhere and whose advice, on some isolated matter, Whitehall pressed the men-on-the-spot to heed. Since the age of colonial emancipation, social philosophers have dominated our intellectual world. One can no longer keep up with the accelerating kaleidoscope of their new (or dusted-off) -isms of 'perception' and 'cognition': Functionalism, Structuralism, Lévi-Straussism, Lévi-Bruhlism, the New Marxism, and above all Phenomenologism – Husserlites, Schutzites, and, beyond them, the anti-Schutz Gormanites; their contemporary advocates claim you cannot observe exotic peoples unless schooled in each one's newly-refined system of 'perception'. One might expect the name Phenomenologism to betoken empiricism, but not a bit of it: like their mighty guru, Kant, who never clapped eyes on any phenomenon located more than a dozen miles from Königsberg, the Phenomenologists are Cartesians and reject the reality of what you or I behold, recognizing, if I get their message right, only the 'apodictic truth' revealed exclusively to an abstract 'transcendental ego' in whose understanding of what life feels like for alien peoples we can only share if, by espousing Phenomenology, we make ourselves part of that 'ego'. I have heard it suggested that the customs and problems of Asian peoples can only be understood by sociologists uncontaminated by familiarity with those peoples' languages, and I myself was told one day that I have been cut off for ever from accurate perception of Chinese life by my earlier involvement in it. I felt that day like Bernard Shaw's Black Girl wandering through the jungle from one

missionary to another in search of God . . . and wished I had
her knobkerrie!

If my 'cohabitation' with Overseas Chinese people as a colonial
administrator in the 1950s does have any relevance, it is less
for the positive perceptions of their life then, than for the
prompting of observation on my tour in 1979. Few of my
colleagues in government have recorded their experience in
office; the outstanding one in perception of Chinese self-
perception, so to speak, is, in my opinion, *Myself a
Mandarin – the Memoirs of a Special Magistrate*, by Austin
Coates.[5] The relationships and attitudes of the common folk
of the New Territories of Hong Kong in the 1950s, as revealed
in the disputes that came before Coates for settlement, though
reported entertainingly, have an authentic ring which no
school of social philosophy can discredit in the eyes of the
reasonable reader. There are two recollections of my own
duties in Malaya at that time which kept coming into my mind
in 1979.

The first recollection is of interviewing Chinese applicants
in Singapore for naturalization as British subjects under the
British Nationality Act of 1948 on the eve of devolution of
power and the introduction of a constitution for self-
government. The purpose of naturalization was less otiose
than it may sound, coming at such a late stage of colonial rule,
for many Chinese residents of Singapore had been born
either in China or in other parts of Southeast Asia, and a
procedure was necessary by which to enfranchise them and
give them a say in the political future of their adopted
homeland. Needless to say, a sudden access of loyalty to the
King was hardly the motive of any of the applicants; instead it
was the threat to their way of life that arose from the
combination of the Red Army's victory in China and the fact
or prospect of colonial emancipation throughout Southeast
Asia. Until after the Second World War, the Chineseness of
their race and – though many were poorly educated – of their
culture was something they could understand, but nationality
was a new and perplexing concept. All occupations, gainful
and rentier, were represented among the men, and a few
women, who sat in front of me under the lethargic ceiling fan

on those sweltering afternoons. Scores of the well-to-do *towkays* (merchants) were heads of extended families; they had a branch managed by a son – occasionally the son's mother as well, one of several wives – in Rangoon and in Penang, in Pontianak and Padang, in Manila and Surabaya, amongst which they moved themselves, their goods and their capital at will to catch the market. Until after the Second World War, all three kinds of movement were free and unfettered in the region, and Southeast Asia had been the Chinese towkays' oyster. Now, suddenly, the 'self-determination' of Burma, the Philippines, Indochina, Malaya and Indonesia – the last still unpredictably about to become one or possibly three 'new Nations' – were all imposing tariffs and exchange controls, and demanding passports (with threat of visas to come) and 'national' registration of businesses. Soon the towkays might not only lose their livelihood, but the network of their family affections and their identity as well. Beyond a sympathy as sincere as I could make it sound, all I had to offer them, as representative of an empire prostrate from victory in a world war, was the flimsy certificate of naturalization. After thirty years, had the threat to their quality of life materialized?

My second recollection is of a single case four or five years earlier. I was stationed at Ipoh, in an imposing Malay *astana* built of teak and still called at that time the Chinese Protectorate. One of my duties was to arbitrate in Chinese labour disputes and family disputes; I wore the usurped mantle of a mandarin (a *tai jin* in Malayan parlance), but my arbitrations had no binding force. Mostly I tussled with communist trade unions bent on 'creating a revolutionary situation' in the tin and rubber industries of the neighbourhood – it was before the people's war began – but one of the family cases stands out in my memory. An Indian, a middle-aged Chinese couple, a young Chinese obviously the woman's son, and an adolescent Chinese girl, not pretty but conspicuously pregnant, were ushered in by an interpreter and sat down with formal shyness.[6]

It took half an hour to worm out their relationship; they could well have been Five Characters in Search of an Author. The girl turned out to be a *mui tsai* – that is to say, she had been bought illegally in infancy from her parents, now disappeared, to grow up a servant round the house and at

puberty become a 'second wife' to the son – a 'passage' in the
mui tsai's life often marked only by the perfunctory 'rite' of
being told to sleep from tomorrow night onwards in the son's
bed instead of on the outhouse floor. Knowing no alternative
course of action, the girl had obeyed. But there was a Hindu
school next door, and a few months later she had been
seduced by a new teacher, the Tamil in front of me – a man, I
noted, of less attractive features and bearing than the jilted
son. Over and over I was enjoined by the mother's shrill voice
to command the *kei nui* (the strumpet) to return to the son's
bed forthwith. Neither boy nor girl – utterly wretched, both
of them – uttered a word; she just kept shaking her head,
while he brooded miserably. Although the Tamil could not
marry the *mui tsai* because he was a Christian and had a wife in
India, he refused to renounce her: her baby was his, he said.
But the parents of the cuckolded boy insisted the baby was *his*.

It took another half hour to get an oblique allusion to the
crucial fact: the parents had realized that their son (an only
child) was probably impotent, and the only way to conceal the
shameful truth and get another family to part with its
daughter as a principal wife for him and daughter-in-law for
themselves was to have the girl's baby born in their house,
hope it was male and not too dark-skinned, and make believe
their son had begotten it. The baby might in any case be their
only hope of a grandson, however unsatisfactory his antece-
dents, to sweep their graves in after years. I took a dislike to
the seducer and suspected he was only after the fair-skinned
girl, but the rest of them were locked in tragedy. What
settlement would a genuine mandarin have made? I had no
idea: all I could do was make sure the girl understood that, in
Malaya, she owed obedience to none of the others and offer
her the shelter of the *Po-leung Kuk* or welfare home for
'threatened women'. I heard afterwards that she went back to
the family. The quality of that girl's life left room only for
improvement over the next thirty years; but has it changed in
fact for her daughters or for their cousins in the brave New
China?

Observation of Chinese life by study at a distance has been
affected for all observers by the fact that, for most of its first

three decades, the Chinese People's Republic[7] has been closed
to inquiring foreigners, and even the handful who lived there,
as diplomats or as servants of the authorities, were cut off
from making Chinese friends; nor, for twenty years, did the
communist government publish any information about
economic or social conditions. In consequence, two schools of
thought about communist China arose in the West: that of the
China-watchers and that of the Mao-sympathizers. The
'watchers' included university dons, pressmen and foreign
government agencies who, for their several practical purposes, tried, separately or in collaboration, to work out the
facts about contemporary China from indirect evidence. A
select few of the 'sympathizers' who were more reliable in
Chinese eyes (that is, less observant or less critical) were
allowed to visit the People's Republic from time to time, in
order to give their writing a touch of what broadcasters call
'actuality', but all of them, whether thus favoured or not,
agreed that it was morally wrong to want to find out more
about a 'socialist' state than the rulers wanted known;
moreover, in so far as the 'watchers' very frequently were
concerned with questions of defence in the Cold War, their
observations were doubly vitiated and bound to result in
analyses that unwarrantably belittled economic and social
achievements under Marxist–Leninist rule. Which school's
'perception' was right? A recent study in *The China
Quarterly* – the pages of which have published the views of
both schools all the time – has compared the estimates of
industrial and agricultural production given out by various
groups of 'watchers' with figures given out by the Chinese
Government in the last year or two, since the reopening of
intercourse with the West. It shows that China's economic
performance in the heyday of Mao Tsê-tung was, if anything,
feebler than the majority of China-watchers had worked out,
and that the nearest of the latter to hitting on the truth –
nearer than the Russians, who changed sides from being
'sympathizers' when the Sino-Soviet dispute grew acute – was
the CIA, notwithstanding that the most disparaging inten-
tions of all had been ascribed to it by the 'sympathizers'.[8]

In addition to these detective successes in penetrating the
bamboo curtain, there have been other kinds of compensation
for its concealments. Difficulties of communication in

China – about which more will be said in a later chapter – have led to a style of public administration depending largely on statements and reports in the national and provincial press, which are then read out *in extenso* over the broadcasting network, sometimes more than once a day. The immediate worldwide circulation through the FBIS (Federal Broadcast Information Service, US Government) and the SWB (Summary of World Broadcasts, BBC) of monitoring reports of these internal communications has, for all the information's being confined to Chinese Government spokesmen who were at times (as also we shall see later) liars, paradoxically furnished an instant and comprehensive source not to be had for the study of other countries completely open to reporters from the foreign press. For years and years, the US Consulate-General in Hong Kong issued extracts from the contents of periodicals published 'on the mainland' but not monitored from broadcasts; many studies of conditions under the communist regime would never have been commissioned had it not been for the bamboo curtain – for example, the CIA's magnificent *Administrative Atlas*, recording thirty years of internal boundary changes. By contrast with the People's Republic, it has proved in some ways difficult to find out about Chinese life on Taiwan or in Southeast Asia: one is perfectly free to go and see for oneself, but, in the absence of the FBIS and the SWB and the China-watching fraternity, one does have to do so – there is no handy substitute by which to avoid the expense and fatigues of personal travel. As a result, a visit nowadays to Taipei, though touristically less thrilling, can in a sense be more a chance of a lifetime than a visit to Peking, on which sources of information are available at nearly every station bookstall in Europe.

Another bonus from the bamboo curtain has come through stories of occasional Overseas Chinese visitors and above all illegal emigrants from the People's Republic hiding in Hong Kong and discreetly interviewed there by China-watchers; both their flight and the interest in listening to them have been the results of the Mao regime's self-isolation. The Mao-sympathizers have generally denigrated the interview techniques American dons have worked out for getting the whole truth from the emigrants and nothing but the truth; the critics have questioned especially the wide extent of persecu-

(a)   Cantonese matron.

(b)   Temple of Heaven.
1   The China that does not change.

2 Beachcombers of Macau: *(above)* in 1839 and *(below)* at the same spot in 1979.

3 Prosperous days in Cholon before Liberation.

4 Begging for refuge in Hong Kong, April 1979.

5   Precious Lotus Monastery, Hong Kong: *(above)* vegetarian nuns 'Welcome Everybody' in 1949; *(below)* the manager-bonze waits at the 'cathedral' for package trippers in 1979.

6 '. . . extended the pool and built a pavilion where I could come with the people for recreation . . .'

7 'Self-reliant' wheelbarrow invented in Great Leap Forward days.

8 '. . . dragon-roofed pavilions and rugged artificial mountains . . .' (the Yü Garden, Shanghai).

9 This 'piglet' has found Longevity and Happiness, but hardly Fortune.

10 Bat-wing sails before the east wind in Shanghai's deserted dockland.

11 The Buddha the Communist Party built
at Hangchow to further diplomacy with Japan
in the Cold War.

12 Trawler from a Pearl River fishing commune.

13   At the crossroads in Shanghai.

14   Young 'rusticates' demonstrate in Shanghai.

tion at the height of the Mao Tsê-tung dictatorship, during the Great Proletarian Cultural Revolution ten years ago, disclosed in accounts such as *The Revenge of Heaven (Red Guard* in the British edition), which had been told to Miriam and Ivan London of the City University of New York by a refugee calling himself 'Ken Ling'. In spite of the doubt cast on it, that young man's story was confirmed by chance in 1980, in the province where most of it took place (that of *Elegant Flower*), by officials who, knowing nothing of the book, were designated by the Communist Party to talk to a visiting correspondent from the *Washington Post*.[9] Indeed, no less an authority than Chairman Hua Kuo-fêng has in recent months put at a hundred million – twelve per cent of the population – the number of men and women who suffered physical or moral damage in those years of studied cruelty, and at four hundred thousand the number who were butchered. In the social field as well as the economic, therefore, the record of the China-watchers was not more derogatory of the Party than the facts subsequently acknowledged – or alleged – by the Party itself. A Canadian official has remarked how much more he was able to 'perceive' of conditions of life in China from interviewing refugees for a few months in Hong Kong than from all his years of residence in Peking – and what is more important, the degree to which the refugees' stories told to him have been borne out by the Party disclosures.[10]

Admittedly, impressions gathered from air travel, even of simple and obvious things, are patchy and superficial. In the first place, one has to overlook the annoyances: an hour queuing in tropical heat in a stuffy immigration shed at Kuching, not because you are a foreigner or your papers are not right, but because everybody in front of you is a citizen of the country, and it is local nationals, especially Chinese ones, not yourself, who are not allowed to travel from West to East Malaysia without accounting for their journey. Or again, you are obliged repeatedly to turn your luggage out while officials rummage for arms, for drugs, and (with special surliness in Taipei) for 'girlie magazines'. In Korea one is challenged with 'Have you any antlers in your suitcase?' – presumably for conservationist reasons. (Thirty years ago, one was similarly asked at the docks in Singapore 'Have you any corpses about you?' That provision was dictated by the Overseas Chinese habit of repatriating their dead, sometimes without waiting for the preliminaries of decomposition in the sort of temporary grave that was customary at home.) One has to smother the antipathy to a place that surges up when the local airline misroutes your luggage or there are no taxis to take you into town.

The modern hotel circuit is rather an .obstacle to close-up views of local life. Time was when travellers arrived by ship and put up at boarding houses; Somerset Maugham taught us to mock at them wasting their evenings in wicker chairs on creaky verandahs, emptying a whisky bottle as if it were an hourglass. My first recollections are of those days. But I am sure that it was easier to absorb local colour from, let us say, the Eastern Hotel on the Bangkok river front, with its shanghai-jars and thunder-boxes ('And is there pommelo still for tea?'), than from its present-day successor of darkened glass and chromium, shut in and air-conditioned and so standardized that, like Monsieur Hulot on his holiday, one might as well be in Milwaukee as in Bali or Kyoto.

The change in travel in the People's Republic is just as marked if different. When I was free to roam round South China on my own in the 1940s, travel was by 'tow-boat'; these were barges propelled by a tug lashed alongside and were hung with brilliant streamers and banners (coloured neon signs at night) proclaiming the auspiciously-coded names of craft and upstream destinations, and the wrinkled skippers stridently bidding for custom (my favourite was a peg-leg whose surname, appropriately, was pronounced *peet* in Cantonese), made the pre-Liberation Pearl River at Canton one of the gayest scenes I have known. On board there were no open decks, and apart from the cramped central dining-space, you had to squat or lie twenty-four hours a day, under a four-feet ceiling, on a straw mat, each in a two-foot 'narrow cell' and separated cheek from jowl by a companionable, three-inch high, partition. Ablutions twice a day were from brass bowls dipped in the river at the ship's bows and brought to each mat by a girl, to be collected again and tipped back at the stern; for your teeth, you got a brass mugful of the same liquor and gargled the residue into the cuspidor at the end of your mat.

You could penetrate inland from the river ports for remoter sightseeing, by ramshackle bus or sideways on a bicycle carrier, and spend the night in an inn lit by reeking oil lamps, under a stuffy mosquito net the efficiency of which owed more to its unwashed grime than to its fraying threads; you could flair what the dunghills of our own medieval towns must have smacked of. Crouched on a hard stool at a communal round table over a dinner of frog's legs and spinach from the fields, on board or on terra firma, I used to understand at best half of what the other travellers joked about over our shared litres of Shantung beer but, along with the vermin, I picked up generous helpings of 'quality of life'. Alas, in 1979, only two or three towboats were still moored at Canton, but stripped of banners and neon lights and of wharfside throng. We journeyed by tight-fitting Ilyushin, or in an antimacassared reserved coach on the train, and stayed at one French hotel from the 1930s, which Chinese people were not allowed into even when invited by foreign guests, and at three Russian-built hotels no less remote from the people – one of them (in Canton again) grubby and ill-kept, but in a jaded foreign, not a native, way. I thought of that notice in a Shanghai park before Liberation (apocryphal but given currency by the Communist International in *Inprecor*), 'No dogs, no Chinese'; Shanghai today has no dogs left to keep out of the hotels along with the Chinese visitors.

In the People's Republic one faces another hazard of perception as well. Before I left London, China-watcher friends impressed on me the special pitfalls of generalizing from what I would be shown: barely one in a thousand of the communes, they said, has ever felt the tread of a foreign foot. I remember for myself the distinguished lady professor of economics who, several years ago, told us that one sign of the new honesty generated by Marxist rule under Chairman Mao was that 'you could park your car with the keys in it for any length of time and never have it stolen' – quite overlooking that hardly anybody in the People's Republic knew how to drive and that there was not a single privately-owned car in the whole country anyway; or the professor of geography who observed with approval that 'social services are regarded as a basic responsibility of industry to its workers' – a statement that could have been taken at its face value in Taiwan or Hong

Kong, but when applied to the mainland ignored the fact of collective ownership under which 'industry' and 'its workers' were the same people, so that the policy really meant saying to the workers: 'If you want social services, shift for yourselves.'

I have read the disclosures in Simon Leys's *Chinese Shadows*[11] of the tricks invented to impress foreign professors, as well as the allegations of Edward Luttwak that Mao Tsê-tung's Gang of Four got up to elaborate frauds in order to dupe ingenuous American celebrities; yet when my wife and I arrived there, we were treated to no chicaneries half so resourceful as the make-believe Mongolian commune of gaily-coloured yurts under which the sceptical Luttwak noticed the grass was green from yesterday's dew. It was in vain that all thirty-nine of us on our tour pleaded – to the point of being rebuked as 'undisciplined' – to be taken to any truly rural commune, however well-trodden: all we saw was Simon Leys's suburban tea-estate at Hangchow and a market-garden in greater Shanghai, though both called themselves communes. Our tour was less expensive than Luttwak's, the hoodwinking proportionately simpler and more innocent: a family showed off its typical home, but a second look at the kitchen revealed that no meals had ever been cooked in it; shepherded through a little handicrafts factory in Peking, those of us who turned back suspiciously had a door slammed in our faces just as the suspect workers got up from their benches. In a textile mill, one tourist asked to inspect the lavatories and reported them wholesome; he had been shown the management's – the workers' place, which I got wind of, was every bit as noisome as the provincial inns in the old days.

It was with our minds fully alerted to all these cautions and possible criticisms that my wife and I set out with our bags, through the snowdrifts of the East Kent winter, for the *terra cognita* of the Chinese world.

2 Socialist Transformation and Economic Miracle

'Not till the granaries are full should one talk about moral uplift.'

(Ancient Chinese maxim)

If change in the quality of Chinese Man betokens change in the quality of his life, the 'socialist transformation' which the Chinese Communist Party proclaims for the former ought to have wrought profound change in the latter. Analogous change is implied in talk of 'the economic miracle' in Taiwan and Hong Kong and Singapore – less certainly in Southeast Asian countries where the Chinese are a minority. Under Mao Tsê-tung's 1954 Constitution (no longer in force), the tactics of socialist transformation were economic – the Marxian 'unleashing of the forces of production captive under the old, capitalist, regime', especially in agriculture; but the strategic aim behind socialist transformation was social engineering to produce the new Socialist Man, presumably in the engineer's (Mao's) own somehow pre-transformed image. I share the opinion of Professor Lifton[1] that Mao worried over the 'immortality' of his social achievement; but I would go further than he does. It was logical that Mao should view his own despotism as Party Leader in the same way as Lenin viewed the dictatorship of the Party itself: the will of Party or Leader must take absolute precedence in the state over every other consideration, person or interest, lest the high goal of the revolution (fulfilment of the 'laws' Marx laid down for History to follow) should be compromised in the least respect. In state policy, Mao's exemplar was Stalin, during the latter's declining years when he was pursuing metaphysical immortality as the 'transformer of Nature' by applying the biological theory

15

of Ivan Michurin, urged on him by the sycophantic Lysenko. Michurin had asserted that biological species can be transformed by environmental change and that characteristics thus acquired will be transmitted by heredity. Michurinism lent support to Lysenko's wishful proposition that varieties of grain 'improved' by its methods would multiply the harvests, whereas those 'unleashed forces of production', frankly, had not. Could the theory not apply to human society as well as the vegetable kingdom? The intimidatory campaigns of communist rule in China, from the Land Reform to Mao's Stalinesque apotheosis in the Great Proletarian Cultural Revolution and after, would not only liquidate the despot's past opponents and cow anybody minded to oppose him in future, but would so mould the contemporary generation's political culture that the pattern would be passed on to future generations. I call the idea Social Michurinism on the analogy of Herbert Spencer's Social Darwinism – which declares that wealth accrues by natural laws innate in society to the socially fittest – which Mao had studied in his youth, and which Western Marxists tell us is the dominant socio-philosophical doctrine in the lands of the economic miracle. Social Michurinism gave Mao hope that he could make his regime immortal – a 'permanent revolution' in a sense not envisaged by Trotsky when he coined that phrase: rendered pliant by a succession of 'cultural revolutions', the Chinese people singly and collectively would henceforward behave economically–socially–politically according to the correct line for ever and ever and enable the state to wither away, as foretold by Engels.

Mao died in 1976, but had he really left behind an undying mark on the obvious things of life – on people's clothes, their houses, the traffic in the streets? And how did these things differ in the other Chinese communities, which had escaped his proletarianizing revolution?

There is not much distinctive charm about the style of Chinese clothes anywhere nowadays. Except for the summery *ch'eung sam* of Hong Kong ladies, the magyar cut, with fastenings by thread loops over minute silk buttons, has largely gone out in favour of the set-in sleeve and buttonholes of European costume. Girl tin-miners in Malaya still keep the sun off their complexions with tight-wristed sleeves and red scarves under conical straw hats, and in Hong Kong women's bamboo boaters with black curtains round the rim survive in a few villages where the peasant pursuits they make more comfortable survive; I noticed one or two of them from the train on the China side of the frontier as well. Modernization of Chinese dress no doubt goes with better living conditions: thirty years ago, working people in South China and Southeast Asia, men and women alike, chiefly wore a black silk stuff with sateen finish that was hard to wash, and often went noticeably unwashed; when in a warm climate there are more incentives to look clean, then fast-coloured cotton is more practical. But additional, constraining, factors have been at work on Chinese fashions. In Indonesia, the Philippines and Malaysia it does not pay for Chinese people to stand out the way they used to like to do in colonial times; in flowered shirts or frocks they can blend with other races on neutral, international, ground, so to speak. In Malaysia, it is the Malay and Indian womenfolk who still wear clothes characteristic of their race; local-born Chinese women used to have their own variant on the Malay two-piece (*baju China*), but there are fewer of them around now. In Indonesia it is difficult to pick out Chinese men and women in the street in the towns of Java.

Changes of fashion like that among the Overseas Chinese are a question of personal choice – at most of social pressure, and certainly not of direction by the government. In People's China, on the other hand, it is obvious that there has been no personal choice and that such variety as appears in the streets today is recent. The standard is the buttoned-up two-piece worker-suit of blue denim, worn by men and women alike, and also, in khaki, by soldiers; in fact it originated in the fatigues that Lenin wore in his last year or two, that Sun Yat-sen adopted, that the Red Army lived in on its legendary Long March in 1935, and that the Party leaders were wearing when they became masters of the towns and never found the right moment to stop wearing, and that has permeated to the lowest ranks of society in the way the sola topi has done in the Third World. It is cheap to mass-produce and launder, and even unfetching air hostesses sport it. For Sunday-go-to-meetings 'best', both men and women match the denim with that comradely cloth cap which, ever since Friedrich

Engels went to work in the Manchester mill his family owned,
has symbolized working-class rectitude in the socialist world.
Gone are the old black silk caps of the men shaped like a
cardinal's hat, and gone are the trilby hats I remember men of
all classes used in China's bourgeois days to wear incongru-
ously with magyar-cut, ankle-length gowns of Manchester
worsted for winter or of grey silk for summer (cotton for the
poor). Gone are the rags and threadbare smocks that were
common in Peking in the 1940s. No bare feet – but then there
were none before: the soft felt bedroom slipper, tight round
the top of the foot and ankle, is still the footwear in vogue, for
soldiers too off duty. The gracelessness of Communist Party
basse couture is being relaxed, if one can judge from the
shop-windows of 'progressive' Shanghai. In the ladies' and
gentlemen's outfitters I spotted, in take-it-or-leave-it Peking,
whether in traditionally-built shops or on the ground floor of
new concrete blocks of flats, you had to go inside to see the
little-varied readymades; but the shop-windows of Shanghai,
which date from the 1930s, beckoned with a choice of styles in
denim or gaberdine dyed brown, grey or beige instead of blue.
Even in Shanghai, however, the only variant of cut the tailors
seemed to know was to open the neck with short lapels for a
shirt underneath – though I did not notice any ties. In the
freezing weather of Peking latitudes, people were still wearing
cotton-padded jackets in the countryside, Russian-looking
padded denim overcoats in the town, with fleece-lined denim
caps (fur-lined at three times the price).

What does the uniformity of dress associated with socialist
transformation imply? It is the consequence of deliberate
levelling, for the cardinal sin in communist ethics is individuality, and Party leaders still set the same tone by always being
photographed in worker-suits. Yet even before the partial
relaxation began, they probably always stopped short of the
rigid enforcement by regulation which in imperial times
governed, for example, the wearing of pigtails as a badge of
Chineseness, contrariwise, to distinguish (not identify) the
mass of the people *vis-à-vis* their Manchu rulers; conformity
will have been achieved after 1949 primarily through limitation of supplies in the shops. Nor is uniformity a new feature
of Chinese life: there never was a great deal of latitude in
Chinese dress, and the predominance of blue for town wear,

together with its special significance as mourning, was noted already by Dyer Ball as long as eighty years ago.[2] As against that, although I have not seen it suggested that having to dress alike has been one of the curbs on personal liberty most felt by the masses in the People's Republic, it is a fact that, as soon as stocks of more interesting clothes came on the market a little before my visit, they were snapped up and intellectuals disgraced under the Cultural Revolution but since rehabilitated and allowed to come abroad as 'delegates' have taken to European clothes again, as if to suggest that the worker-suit is becoming the uniform of Party cadres.

The Chinese traffic in the non-communist Far East comprises the same cars, buses and lorries as traffic in Europe and America, criss-crossing by flyovers and underpasses and out onto rural motorways all as characterless as Monsieur Hulot's hotels. In out of the way spots like East Malaysia, you can still ride in a Chinese 'pedicab'. In my early days, the pedicab constituted a technological advance on the Japanese 'man-power carriage' (the *jinrickshaw*). It was an advance to the extent that impressionable foreigners had judged the 'rickshaw' degrading for the coolie who pulled it – for the 'human camel' as the rickshaw boy is called in the Chinese title of a once-fashionable Marxist novel by Lao Shê. Long on the index of 'rightist' books, the novel was republished in English (*Rickshaw Boy*) to mark the author's posthumous political rehabilitation during my visit to China; he had been driven to suicide in the Cultural Revolution. A few rickshaws, and palankeens as well (the depths of degradation?), are still kept in bourgeois Hong Kong, not for getting round in, but for rich foreigners off cruise-liners to take each other's picture in. In People's China there are no 'manpower carriages' left even as photo-props, and the real camels, shaggy and supercilious in my faded old snaps, have, with the trams, vanished from the streets of Peking. But there are plenty of manpower *carts*, laden with timber or rubble or stone, dragged through the streets by one, two or more straining stand-ins for camels, women more often than men. Although I saw none myself, a New China News Agency report just after I left China mentioned peasants in one of the provinces being seen harnessed to ploughs for lack of draught animals. Waggons with an outboard tractor-engine stuck in front are an invention of Maoist 'self-reliance' that is to be seen in all the towns. Trolleybuses have taken the place of trams in Shanghai and Hangchow. The few grey motorcars, fitted with coy curtains, are manufactured in People's China, but only for use by officials; the lumbering lorries of Russian design appear to be owned by the army and the government rather than by people's communes or collective enterprises, which are expected to get by with labour-intensive means of transport as far as possible and take up the employment slack. Although, even when one includes the buses, motor vehicles are too few to cause town congestion, they set up a din with their horns to outdo the Canebière in pre-war Marseilles. Not one of the half dozen bus drivers employed during my tour knew how to change gear, and comparative unfamiliarity with the internal combustion engine is one of the striking differences in Chinese life between living under socialism and living under capitalism.

The bicycle is the limit of mechanization for the majority of the masses in China, and more of them use it today than thirty years ago, although the number has grown less fast than that of cars owned by the Overseas Chinese. The butts of the hooting are sometimes the cyclists – swooping from crossroads to crossroads in flocks that look like the pigeons their machines are called after – and sometimes the more numerous pedestrians, for the commonest way of getting about in the town centres is still to walk. Old Peking used to seem to me to be meant for walking in, under Kublai Khan's majestic Mongol walls, the Manchu watchtowers, the Chinese 'gates-of-happy-sparrows', and the wooden arches commemorating long-forgotten triumphs of local boys who made good under the old regimes, imperial or republican. In recent years, those picturesque obstructions have been swept away and boulevards opened up . . . to relieve hoped-for traffic jams, to accommodate million-strong political parades on Sundays, or to safeguard Mao Tsê-tung's citadel of power, as Haussmann's boulevards through Paris opened a field of fire for Napoleon III's bodyguard? Would indeed that China had an Haussmann! Do the Pekingese mind losing their antique surroundings? They dare only answer that 'it was necessary'.

There never was much of the antique in Hong Kong or Taipei or Singapore, and what there is in Bangkok or Djakarta is not Chinese. The quaint feature of Chinese streets that foreigners know best is the 'flowery board' – the shop sign in artistic characters and bright colours hung from upper floors at right angles to the street. Since the 1950s, it has gained a new lease of night-life from the economic miracle by the addition of neon lights of many hues – to such an extent that municipal street lighting is almost superfluous in Taipei or Kowloon or parts of Singapore. One cannot doubt but that the Chinese heart is lightened by the sight of flowery boards, but they are not allowed any more by the native authorities in Thailand or Indonesia. In the People's Republic, one did not see them much thirty years ago in the single-storeyed northern cities, but they have disappeared altogether now, together with the private trade they advertised. The loss must surely be a deprivation for the mass of the people – as, I suspect, is the elimination of food vendors, whose charcoal braziers, rice-bowls and diminutive portable stools are a picturesque amenity for underprivileged pedestrians that spans the decades, if anything with enhanced vitality, this side of the bamboo curtain.

Wherever there are Chinese people, there are crowds; one reason for the crowds perpetually in the streets is overcrowding in the home, and if a Chinese family does not like that, there is no escape for them by crossing the bamboo curtain in either direction. The high-rise estates of Hong Kong and Singapore – introduced in the former in order to get rid of the deeply-insanitary, highly-inflammable and, in typhoon weather, treacherously-steep hillside shanties of the 1950s fugitives from Liberation – are in their infancy in Peking; nearly everybody there still lives in a *hu-t'ung* or alley of single-storey brick compounds, rice-paper instead of glass still in some of the windows (usually giving onto inside yards) and the same old stovepipe chimney belching half-burnt coal dust and acrid gas sideways into the smog just above the faces of pedestrians and cyclists, who wear the same cotton mouth-masks as in pre-Liberation times. (The little piles of coal-dust bricks of the 1940s were no longer in evidence on the pavement near doorways.) From the Yangtze to the equator, the standard Chinese town dwelling is the shophouse with its one or two-cubicled rooms upstairs. In Macau and Semarang, Bangkok and Haadyai, Kuching and Ipoh, I saw little change except for the television aerials and air-conditioners. But in Woosung and Hungk'ou and Chapei, the old Chinese quarters of Shanghai, there were no electrical appliances in sight, and the masses were crammed inside doorways as they were on the pavements; only in the old International Settlement and the French Concession, to both sides of Bubbling-Well Road (not called that nowadays), the European houses keep just a breath of defiant middle-class ease – their ageing residents, in my new snaps, the smug Shanghai bearing of old.

Housing and social structure interact, and in the rural areas of any country family life tends to shape the houses, whereas in cities (more state-controlled) housing shapes family life. The vast housing estates built by the governments of Hong Kong and Singapore in response to the spiralling economic miracle – and in the former crushing everything picturesque or 'environmental' under their concrete heel – are bringing new problems to the East over care of the aged, when grandparents live on one estate, parents and grandchildren on another; housing is breaking down family solidarity. I was told in Peking that such problems are anticipated there too but cause little anxiety yet because family solidarity still holds. Now, the joint family which is traditional in China, the lineage, is a hindrance to socialist transformation, and Mao's acceleration of collectivization in the 1950s towards its 'highest stage', the rural commune, was meant, among other aims, to break it down: peasants were even obliged to abandon their private hearths and to patronize communal kitchens. Yet the new building I could see in villages near Canton, north of Peking, and in the central region was all in local – from the tourist's-eye view, attractive – pre-Liberation styles native to those various regions. Sociologists who since the thaw on foreign intercourse have managed to get into the countryside, at least of South China, have reported robust lineage solidarity in defiance of measures calculated to discourage it; and that solidarity, the sociologists also report, is manifesting itself particularly in the spending of remittances, sent to the peasants for generations past by relatives in economic-miracle countries, on enlargement of the peasants' homes, so that when their children grow up and marry they can be sure of all staying together. If one makes a superficial comparison between Hong Kong and Canton, therefore, Chinese life seems rather to have remained the same under progressive socialism, but to have evolved under reactionary capitalism.

These visual cross-curtain impressions are a measure, it seems to me, of the comparative economic achievement of socialist transformation and the economic miracle. In Singapore and Hong Kong, there is ceaseless urban renewal as improved designs for public housing replace earlier stop-gaps, and it is all paid for out of taxation on labour and enterprise under capitalist management. Evidently, despite the collectivization or nationalization of all the means of production in China proper, peasants and a great many urban workers have to fend for themselves when it comes to housing: although their home is the one substantial asset they can call their own, it is so thanks only to the failure of socialist transformation to yield enough surplus value to match the scale of development in low-cost dwellings of the economic-miracle countries. During my visit to Peking, the New China News Agency was blaming the Party advisers drafted to rural areas for interfering with production instead of improving it – a criticism that might be directed at the whole economy of China, since Chairman Hua Kuo-fêng admitted that half the industrial output was substandard, and a quarter produced at a financial loss. One of the big-character posters I saw was to the point: scrawled, not on Democracy Wall at Peking but on the wall of the Corinthian-column, Throgmorton-Street palace adapted since 1949 to house Party Headquarters on the Shanghai Bund, it read on one line, 'Down with political oppression!' and on the next, 'Down with economic management!'

One has often been told by Mao-sympathizers, 'At least nobody dies of starvation in China today' – a remark surely to be classed with 'At least under Mussolini trains don't run late' . . . and no truer. A group of peasant demonstrators protesting against famine had been chased out of Peking the day before I arrived, and Vice-Chairman Li Hsien-nien was reported just afterwards to have lamented that eleven per cent of the population of China was going short of food. Food shortages resulting from bad weather ('natural disasters'), and under-production resulting from lack of incentive, were a feature of the old regime, and they were aggravated by the civil war while the Red Army was fighting for power – although I never saw the evidence for myself. Thirty years on, this last ill has ceased but the first two continue, according to the unwontedly-candid post-Mao leaders, in spite of so many hopes that socialist transformation would improve both productivity and equable distribution between regions and classes; the rationing that was still in full rigour in 1979 had not had to be introduced until five years after Liberation, and on the eve of my journey the *People's Daily* disclosed that there were many areas producing less for the masses to eat now than they had before Liberation. There seems to be a law of history that Marx overlooked; it is that countries brought under communist party rule cease to be able to feed their population without recourse to grain grown under the capitalist mode of production – in China's case since 1960, grain grown in North America and Australia. Overseas Chinese communities are not generally agricultural, but Taiwan, which is, had, together with the other better-known achievements of its economic miracle, attained self-sufficiency by the late 1960s; however, since 1976 diversion of manpower to industry has led to resumed importation of cereals from North America there too. That even the poorest Chinese person living anywhere *outside* the People's Republic should actually go short of food is unthinkable today.

There is an ethical side to socialist transformation. The claim of Marxists is that their seizure of power is justified, at one level, in the cause of social justice, and certainly one does not see signs in the streets of wide gaps between rich and poor; but I never saw them before Liberation either, and such gaps do not attract one's attention outside mainland China. However, Marxists defend the ruthlessness of socialist transformation, at another level, as a means of wiping out that immorality of personal behaviour which they maintain is inseparable from the 'capitalist system'; Mao and his followers justified socialist transformation in part as a means of eradicating prostitution, drug-peddling, larceny, administrative corruption, fortune-

telling, spirit-mediumship, gambling, and other 'disorder-
linesses', as well as that 'opium of the people' (so called, of
course, because in Marx's day true opium was consumed
openly and respectably by the middle and upper classes of
England as a painkiller, whereas the poor could not afford it),
namely the practice of religion. I imagine drunkenness does
not feature on the communist list of deviances because
Chinese people are not often addicted to it – a fact having
nothing to do with politics. But all the practices that do feature
on the list are blatant among the Overseas Chinese communities, and the more surplus value the economic miracle
transfers to the private hands of the masses the more they
flourish; modern education has made few inroads into belief
in tricks of magic to sway chance, and I confess that the
modern public-relations techniques I helped introduce in
1958 to curb susceptibility to heroin – ironically a 'modernized' refinement of opium – have not prevailed in Hong
Kong, while 'chasing the dragon' (smoking instead of injecting
heroin), I was told, is a growing curse of conscripts in the
Singapore army. Social abuses like the selling of children
mentioned in Chapter 1 have been suppressed by the governments of all those capitalist countries, but in response, it
needs to be said, to a change in attitude by the majority of the
Overseas Chinese public itself – a change, like the abandonment of foot-binding, largely complete, as it was in China
proper as well, before the baseline in time of my comparison.
In the People's Republic, the changes in social structure that
went with the shift in control of the means of production
ought, in Marxian theory, to have cut the ground from under
the feet of the deviants: there is no point in stealing if you
cannot dispose of your haul because there are no markets; no
woman will take to prostitution under conditions of full
employment; when the economy is collectivized there are no
private interests to serve corruptly; and the knowledge of
'scientific socialism' (not to mention 'socialist science') must
destroy at a blow *any* belief in the supernatural, whether
'superstitious' or 'religious'.

In practice, no such moral benefits flowed automatically
from socialist transformation during the first years of communist rule, and the suppression of deviance had to be by
force – not by regulatory and judicial methods, but by

administrative decision and by arbitary punishment – in the last resort in a *gulag* – for what was damned as a form of 'counterrevolution', the Marxian equivalent of medieval European 'heresy'. Final suppression of religion was left to the Red Guards who drove out bonzes and priests and sacked pagodas and churches in execution of the Great Proletarian Cultural Revolution; the devout laity ceased to constitute that spiritual fellowship without which religion cannot be handed down from generation to generation. But no sooner did the overthrow of the Mao faction after the great man's death lead to the relaxation of the repressive apparatus he had instituted than all the execrated deviances reappeared, to the expressed chagrin of Party leaders. I saw nothing of the vice on my tour, although one or two other members unearthed it in Shanghai; its recrudescence is another of the revelations due to the Party's new-found candour, and so too is disclosure of the resurgence of gambling (leading to suicide as an escape from debt), fortune-telling, and most curiously the practice of geomancy. Fear among peasants that infrastructure developments encroaching on their land will alienate spirits of water and weather is one of the most enduring elements in Chinese folklore, and, when I worked for it, the Hong Kong Government used to budget for the hire of spell-breakers to appease the peasants when pipelines had to be built to or from reservoirs or new roads cut across a valley; development plans were constantly being set back because some lineage, advised by geomancers, had buried one of their well-to-do dead on the site and exhumation would amount to desecration. Geomantic protests held up the building of railways in North China under the Manchus, and one of the authors of the book referred to earlier[3] found geomantic precautions to be general if not universal in quite sophisticated surroundings in Taiwan. The latest manifestation on the mainland has been interference with oil prospecting on Hainan Island – threats to the technicians and sabotage of their instruments to the value of 450,000 yüan (£150,000).

The deviance that appears to be constant inside and outside China, and to have remained constant in defiance of Party campaigns to eradicate it, is corruption. Charges of corruption are often false: in the modern world they gain credence very easily, especially in the West about the East, and consequently they offer a plausible charge with which to malign an enemy. Nevertheless, it is as big a fallacy to suppose that corruption is confined to market economies as to suppose that men steal because they are poor. In practice, corruption can sometimes operate as the redeeming feature of tyranny – the one path of escape where all other remedies are denied. In the People's Republic, the ingenious methods of corruption complained of in the Party press are too numerous to list here, but the commonest entail misreporting output and falsifying factory or commune accounts, the culprits usually being persons in authority, the beneficiaries individuals, families, or whole groups of 'transformed' workers. It is obvious, in case after case recounted by refugees and condemned in the Communist Party's provincial press, that the system of control over economy and society lends itself specially to embezzlement, simony, nepotism and graft of a score of kinds. In other words, socialist transformation, far from purifying Chinese society of abuses inherited from capitalism or from what the Party likes to call 'feudalism', actually exposes it to them. But, of course, that is a consideration under the heading of the quality of Chinese Man; whether on balance it is a good or bad thing for his quality of life, and what he thinks about it, are questions I could not probe on my tour.

To my mind, the most dramatic evidence in 1979 of the falseness of claims that socialist transformation has changed the quality of life of Chinese people for the better lay in the fate of the Boat People, whose exodus received new impetus from the Chinese incursion into Vietnam while I was in Peking. The Overseas Chinese in Indochina were one link in the pan-Southeast Asian network of families obliged by colonial emancipation to seek new national allegiances; furthermore, their livelihood was tied at several points to the wholesale rice trade and threatened by any and all the programmes of land reform being advanced by the different native competitors for the succession to French political authority. Unlike the British authorities in Singapore, the French made no provision for the Chinese to have any say in the future of their land of domicile. When the Geneva

Agreements of 1954 partitioned Indochina between communist and non-communist rule, the Chinese domiciled in
Tonkin (the minority) acquiesced in socialist transformation
of their enterprises and their families at the hands of the
Vietnamese Communist Party, aided and advised from Peking. The majority scattered round the rest of Indochina (a
million and a half or so) acquiesced in the second-class
citizenship accorded them by the new non-communist governments in Saigon, Phnom Penh and Vientiane, but at the
same time profited in their livelihood from financial connec-
tions with the booming economies of Hong Kong, Taiwan and
Singapore.

After the Vietnamese People's Army overwhelmed the
other Indochina governments in 1975, the Chinese conquered with them found themselves a shuttlecock of the
socialist transformations of rival Chinese, Vietnamese and
Cambodian Communist Parties, to the cost of the means of
support of all of them and of the actual lives of many
thousands. Finally, after the Vietnamese broke with China in
order to align Indochina more closely, both economically and
politically, with the USSR, the Overseas Chinese were evicted
in large numbers altogether – not only those newly conquered
in South Vietnam, but also the ones long since transformed in
North Vietnam – overland into Thailand or People's China,
or else, together with boatloads of Vietnamese refugees, by
sea to any destination whatever; for thousands whose fate it
was to hail sea captains of the stamp of Conrad's Lord Jim and
who made no landfall, their destination has been the bottom
of the sea. There was a cruel aptness in the term 'boat people',
as for hundreds of years the Vietnamese have called all
Chinese people 'junk folk'; even in respectable literature,
'junk' stands for 'Chink'. Ho Chi Minh's successors in power
first expropriated the Chinese clerks and tailors and
mechanics in South Vietnam, and then offered them for the
future – not as individual undesirables but as a mass condemned by race, culture and creed – conditions of state
serfdom in 'new economic areas', modelled on Stalin's settle-
ments on 'virgin lands' in Siberia – areas that were too barren
for Vietnamese peasants to want to till; the alternative was to
buy their way out of socialist Vietnam with gold or foreign
exchange remitted by friends – even collected by Vietnamese

communist agents from well-wishing co-nationals – in the lands of the economic miracle and destined to be pocketed part by the communist authorities, part (quite openly) by particular cadres. The choice for these unhappy people was between certainly starving and possibly drowning. By comparison with the quality of life of their great-grandfathers, who were called 'piglets' when they sailed out of China a century ago, as indentured coolies, because of the manner in which they were packed into battened-down holds, that of the victims of this Chinese brain-drain in reverse has deteriorated beyond the predictions of their most ominous forebodings.

3   Toilers of the Far East

'The Chinese peasant toils beyond his strength for sixteen or eighteen hours a day, only to see his labour enrich foreign moneylenders and their mercenary lackeys.'

(Manifesto of the First Congress of the Toilers of the Far East,   Petrograd, 1922)

Often compared with the Jews, the Chinese people have always enjoyed a reputation for hard work and thrift. It is equally common to put the economic miracle of Taiwan, Hong Kong and Singapore down to their 'Confucian work ethic'. All of these three economies have benefited from investment of foreign capital – coming in Taiwan, it is true, largely from strategically-motivated American aid, but in Hong Kong and Singapore (which have never been beneficiaries of foreign *aid*) from industrious Overseas Chinese in Indonesia, the Philippines or Malaysia, nervous about their financial future since the removal of the safeguards for freedom of movement and of commerce they believed were dependent on colonial rule. But the greater share of the capital behind the miracle has been formed by local thrift in all three economies, while the rest has been attracted by the 'ethic' by which it was confidently expected the capital invested would be turned into commodities or into profitable services. Until recently, the Chinese Communist Party spurned offers of investment from abroad and, notwithstanding a relaxation of the old opposition at the time of my visit, has tended once again to go back on projects envisaged, perhaps rashly, for those few months. If industriousness really is a national Chinese characteristic, it is tempting to speculate whether, but for Mao's revolutionary principle (or prejudice) in trying to isolate the Chinese economy from the outside world, the economic miracle – or at least the light-industry sector of it – might not have taken place in the People's Republic instead of outside, and with magnified effect on the worldwide balance of international trade: that the capitalist system in Europe would be destroyed in the end by competition from a technically modernized China was one of Engels's predictions.

However that may be, my tour was not concerned with macro-economics but with the position in them of individual men and women. In Marxian eyes, workers are better off in China as things are because, under socialism, they are not exploited 'man by man': although a man may be misled into believing he is better off under capitalism by dint of hiring out his labour to the employer who offers him the best remuneration, he is worse off 'objectively', since the act of hiring himself out makes him a wage slave submitting to exploitation. The logic Marxians apply to the question was explained long ago by Lenin: 'The course of development of all capitalist countries proves only the objective truth of Marx's whole social and economic theory in general, not merely of one or other of its parts; Marx's theory is an objective truth, and by following the path of Marxian theory we shall draw closer and closer to objective truth – by following any other path we shall arrive at nothing but confusion and lies.' According to this 'apodictic' chain of argument – leading, it must be admitted, to a conclusion which is the opposite of Kant's rights-of-man ideals – the facts of individual life are 'subjective' and therefore falsified by the higher Truth of the Marxian system, which a priori is 'objective': freedom to bargain over one's wages is slavery. In the People's Republic, my group was told, the worker does not own his labour – it is owned collectively, and he shares in the collective ownership of everybody else's labour who works beside, above or below him; although the money he receives may be less and buy less than he could expect under capitalism, he is better off 'objectively' because he is not exploited.

Yet agitation inside China since the death of Mao Tsê-tung for a higher standard of living suggests that, whatever the intended effects on their minds of socialist transformation, the workers of China do not view their 'eighteen-hours-a-day' toil quite so metaphysically as the Party does. The following pages consequently concentrate on more materialist criteria for judgement of the Chinese workers' quality of life – on the kind of *subjective* calculation the Deputy Prime Minister of China (Comrade Têng Hsiao-p'ing), on a visit to Hong Kong, told the Governor, according to press reports, continues to attract workers from Kwangtung across the bamboo curtain illegally by the thousand.

The basic factor in the worker's life, even under Marxist rule, is his pay. Comparisons are not straightforward: in the first place, whereas Overseas Chinese pay is in currencies linked to a world market providing ready comparisons, the *jên-min pi* (people's dollar) has no market rate of exchange; and secondly, it is hard to find out what China's workers really receive even in that money. I knew before I set out that industrial wages had been fixed uniformly from the centre and frozen from 1957 to 1977; but there is always the possibility of perquisites not controlled that way, and agricultural workers are mostly employed in collectives where remuneration is not laid down by the government but tied to the collective's output and to the proportion of the yield estimated – in a system of workpoints – to have been contributed by the labour of each member on the payroll. At the Hsin Ching commune (the Shanghai market-garden mentioned in Chapter 1), our visiting group was told that the average earnings came to 467 people's dollars a year, which at the official rate of exchange is about £155; the lowest-remunerated member received a quarter of the average (say £40). However, at the same time, the Shanghai provincial radio was reporting an *average* annual wage for agricultural and industrial workers together – the latter presumably higher than the former – of only 120 dollars, or the 'lowest' figure of £40. According to figures issued by the State Statistical Bureau in 1980 for 1979, the nationwide average wage for workers in state enterprises was 705 dollars (£235) – subject, naturally, to a variation between the lowest and the highest-paid on the national scale of about four times, in theory. On the Dragon's Well tea estate at Hangchow, the mean annual take-home pay was 960 dollars a *family*, the minimum 300 and the maximum 3000 – presumably the manager and an interesting clue to the applicability of the four-times rule on differentials in practice;

but Hangchow Radio was saying the middle rate of earnings for that province came to only 138 a *head*, so that a family on the tea estate would have to have seven bread-winners before it could earn the stated average there. In Manchuria the previous year, agricultural earnings were only 107 dollars a head, in Szechuan as low as 71 dollars. The statistics are something of a Chinese Shadow, to borrow Mr Leys's metaphor.

In the system of two-kind remuneration common in China for many centuries, agricultural workers receive their basic rice rations (657 pounds in 1978) free though unmilled – that is to say, receive them, it now transpires, except when national or regional shortages make it impossible for the authorities to honour the obligation – and they pay no rent on their 'private-plot' vegetable patches; the very division between cash and kind-in-cereals must encourage the diet deficient in meat which the authorities deplore together with all the other shortcomings of the system. It is probably not unfair to conclude that, by and large, cash income from employment, all sectors of the economy taken together, is not much above the equivalent of £60 a head of the working population a year – whatever that means in living standard – notwithstanding an official claim that wages are now rising at seven and a half per cent a year while inflation is held at under two per cent.

Outside China, the lowest wages for Chinese workers are paid in Hong Kong; there the average for an unskilled labourer was £546 in 1978 (eleven times as much as 'across the border'), and for a highly-skilled worker £2540. Comparable figures were not available for Taiwan: however, it is claimed that the national average for industrial workers in the Chinese Republic is £960 a year, for service workers £1400 a year, but I suspect that those are middle rates rather than the total wages bill divided by the total number of wage-earners. Rural incomes in Taiwan must be lower than industrial (although that would not be true, for example, in present-day Japan), as they are in Hong Kong; but universally in Hong Kong, and more often than not in Taiwan, rural families derive additional income from the construction projects and marginal services of the booming industrial sector a bicycle or motor-cycle ride from their fields. In both places, many employers

provide big traditional fringe benefits – free meals and transport to and from work, and in Taiwan, as in Shanghai thirty
years ago, both a small supplement from profit-sharing by way
of a New Year bonus and, sometimes, living quarters too as
an incentive to stick with the firm after training. Although
visible traces of the years when Taiwan was a Japanese colony
have faded during the last thirty years, the characteristic
paternalism of industrial organization, some of which was felt
in Shanghai as well before Liberation, can still be observed in
the factories. In the People's Republic, I did not find workers
getting free food – although they used to in the communal
kitchens during the first years of the agricultural communes,
until the kitchens were shut down because the workers gorged
themselves; I noticed in a textile factory that the women did
not have anywhere to sit down while they ate what they
fetched, and paid for, from the present-day kitchen.

When one moves into Southeast Asia, Chinese wages are
higher again: in Singapore, the work force (not exclusively
Chinese) contains a larger proportion of higher skills, and it is
government policy to force wages up all the time, such is the
strength in resisting pernicious inflation of a general economy
based on an ever-expanding regional market for services
– financial ones, oil refining, engineering – sold to neighbouring countries from whose relative weakness Singapore is
largely insulated at present by its independent statehood.
Average wages and salaries in Singapore match those of
Japan – in other words, they are catching up with British
rates; professional emoluments are higher, being related
more closely to emoluments paid in Australia. In those
neighbouring countries where they are a minority, the
Chinese are fortunate and face only limited competition from
native workers because they still tend, as they did thirty years
ago, to monopolize certain sectors of the employment market.
The efforts that began in colonial times, and were redoubled
after decolonization, to mix the labour force have achieved
little in light industry and shopkeeping generally, and especially in the tin-mining industry of Malaysia. Even in activities
where all races participate, such as rubber-tapping, Chinese
workers maintain a higher wage rate than the other races
thanks to employment solely in all-Chinese firms in which
wages are related to receipts from sale of the product, whereas

Indian tappers tend to work for international companies and Malays to operate only as smallholders, neither group offering any competition that might depress Chinese wages. While standards have been stagnant in China proper, the Overseas Chinese have benefited from the general rise in standards of the developed and developing world into which, through both international markets and political affiliations, paradoxically, they have become *more* closely integrated economically than they were in colonial times. The external signs of the rise are not only Western clothes, motorcars and motorways, refrigerators and television sets (which, I have seen it said, cost a tenth of the proportion of average earnings in Taipei of the proportion they cost in Shanghai), but include container ports and well-planned new towns the amenities of which – adieu geomancy! – unquestionably represent a spectacular advance in the timespan of barely a generation. As one flies over Kaohsiung in Taiwan or looks out from a skyscraper in Singapore over the industrial complex of Jurong, the sneer of the Russians (echoed endlessly in the lecture-theatres of Western universities but no longer from Peking) that this integration with world markets, knowing no national boundaries, is 'neocolonialist' sounds paltry.

The pay packet is not the sole factor in the worker's quality of life; working conditions contribute hardly less to his wellbeing and to that of his dependants. Legislation to control Chinese conditions in the colonial territories of Southeast Asia began after the First World War but did not reach its full extent of regulation – welfare, workman's compensation, safety, contracts of service, freedom to combine in unions, etc. – until after the 1941–5 War. In Indochina it lapsed progressively with the enlargement of communist party rule; in Indonesia it remained static, although agencies for enforcement did not always remain intact; in Malaysia and Singapore it underwent amplification and further refinement; Hong Kong and Macau, slower to legislate in this field at the outset because nearer to the Chinese mainland, have gradually caught up with the better international standards laid down in the conventions of the International Labour Organization. The mainland still does not regulate conditions of work by

legislation; but the government of Taiwan provides for
workman's compensation by law, and for other aspects of
industrial welfare through regulations decreed by various
ministries responsible for planning the different kinds of
production.

   Despite these discrepancies from country to country, resulting in the main from differences in the style of public
administration, an eight-hour day or shift has always been the
practice in factories set up by Chinese enterprise, whether at
home or overseas. Reduction of the longer hours worked in
shops to meet the factory standard has proceeded slowly –
more slowly in Hong Kong than in the People's Republic,
where consumers have less money to spend so that it is not
worth keeping shops open late and, no less important, where
there is no resident private owner and the workers do not
receive their meals on the premises at his expense, as they tend
to in Hong Kong and in Southeast Asia. When I first went to
the East, a seven-day week was also common practice, for
weeks and days of the week did not feature in the Chinese
calendar, and the chief relief from the daily round was
provided by irregular feast days at local temples. Nowadays,
Chinese workers anywhere in the Far East find themselves
required to labour at most a six-day week, although it was
implied in a Shantung radio statement on 25 March 1978 that
male commune workers could only count on two rest days a
month and must work overtime on the land gratis to make up
for the other two.[1] The rest day for Overseas Chinese is almost
universally Sunday, since that is the day now recognized by
Theravada Buddhists in Thailand, Burma and Cambodia;
even where Islam is strong – in Malaysia and Indonesia –
Friday is often a day of worship without being a day of rest.
The rest day in China is the international Sunday for all
administrative and management employees and for teachers,
but it is staggered through the week for shop assistants and
transport, mining and factory workers; as it is common in the
towns for husbands and wives, and sometimes adolescent
children, to be employed in different sectors, it is rare for
them to be able to go out together, and I noticed that this was
about the only point over which tourist guides were prepared
to voice regret at the conditions they worked under. In
addition to Sundays, Overseas Chinese workers all get eight or

ten paid public holidays a year, depending on the country
(national days, Chinese New Year, Christmas, Id-al-Fitr, and
so on), and a minimum paid annual holiday of seven days (in
English-speaking countries, laid down by law) – longer with
good employers; on the mainland, under socialism, there are
a dozen or more public days off that are paid for – and then it
is possible for families to go out together – but no annual
holiday. Compulsory demonstrations are usually held on
Sundays.

The comparison unfavourable to the People's Republic
implied here might be answered by saying that holidays sound
desirable, but if the worker lives under cramped conditions
they are little help unless he has somewhere to go with his
family or friends. Crowds mooching along the streets, stop-
ping to read the *People's Daily* in glass wall-cases spaced out
along the thoroughfares – for only one copy of all national
and provincial newspapers reckoned together is printed per
hundred of the population, and there are no news stands in
China – or to stop in front of the posters on the 'democracy
walls', or to watch any trivial street incident or curiosity,
presumably do not have anywhere definite to go and do not
feel the urgent and absorbing 'industrious' purposes which
make the streets of the Overseas Chinese such scenes of hurry
and bustle. Cinemas are open in China all day long, but tickets
are sold through factories and mass organizations instead of a
box-office, so that a black market is generated and frequently
causes obstruction in the street outside; elsewhere cinemas are
usually shut in the morning. The open-air amenities of
Peking – the Imperial Palace, the Temple of Heaven, the
Summer Palace, the Zoo – are much as they were thirty years
ago, for the opening of the first three to the public goes back to
the warlord days soon after the overthrow of the Manchus;
grandfathers explain it all to little granddaughters muffled in
podgy padded tunics – adults in miniature, like English
children in King Charles's day – and young soldiers snap each
other with 1946 cameras in front of the lucky lions with heads
like King Charles spaniels. But two of the central lakes, which
were part of the Imperial City before Mao had the walls
knocked down and were open to the public when I went there
before, are now the headquarters of the Communist Party and
the residence of senior leaders, so they have been taken out of

the pool of public amenities. I found it hard to believe the authorities' claim that there are six times as many trees in Peking today as thirty years ago; I would have thought there might, on the contrary, be fewer. The press has recently voiced discontent over the closing of pre-Liberation parks in the provinces as well.

In Shanghai, in contrast, the little parks of the French Concession and the International Settlement, modelled if anything on railed-in, sandy Paris parks rather than on the open, grassy ones of London, have been added to by the opening of one or two former private parks – for example, the Yü-lineage Garden. We were taken there, and, as we moved among the contented faces of the shoulder-to-shoulder throng of young people on their one day off, slowly winding their way along the narrow, zig-zagging footpaths and over the humped bridges, through dragon-roofed pavilions and between dwarf but rugged artificial mountains and lotus-littered ponds-for-lakes, I felt there was before our eyes an unchanging aspect of the Chinese temperament, old or new, proletarian or bourgeois. It was a marvellous gift of escaping mentally from pressing neighbours and daily drudgery, by sheer dint of imagination focused on the make-believe of a Nature cunningly contrived – of an apodictic Nature, one might say, truer in their mind's eye than nature in the wild. There came into *my* mind the much-read description of China's *idéal jardin*, composed almost two hundred years ago by an out-of-office clerk who lived at Soochow, not many miles from the Yü Garden:

> When laying out a garden with pavilions, bowers, winding pergolas, and orangeries mingled with rocks and flowering shrubs, one should make small things look big, big things look small – make the unreal look real and the real look unreal. You do not need to spend a lot of money or labour in order to make the objects alternately catch the eye and go out of sight. You can dig a hole and make a hillock out of it, fit in rocks to jut out of it, and plant flowers to grow out of it; live plum-fronds will make a fence, and, if there is a wall, cover it with creeper. That way, where actually there is an uninteresting flatness, you can imagine a hill. In the more open spaces, plant quick-growing bamboos and train

plums with thicker branches in front to suggest delicateness where there is bulk. To give an impression of bigness to a little yard, align the walls gently in and out, cover them with green ivy, and set in a slab of stone with chiselled-out characters to look like an inscription; that way, whenever you open your window [panes made of rice-paper cannot be seen through], you will seem to look out over a mountain range of cliffs and hollows stretching away as far as the eye can see. Make an apparently blind alley lead suddenly into an open space, and let a cupboard door give onto an unexpected yard, so that the real is come upon in the unreal. Put a door where there is no way out, with a few bamboos and rocks in front and a little balustrade along the top of the wall to suggest a roof garden, and then you have the unreal looking real.[2]

Leisure amenities in Taipei are not dissimilar to those of Shanghai. The cinemas show international as well as non-communist Chinese pictures, and in place of the palaces of Peking the masses can see the art treasures that used to be housed in them but are now on show in a huge new museum built to palace proportions. Instead of Shanghai's (or Soochow's) gardens, there is a huge public park with water-falls and artificial glades in traditional taste and including one feature that is not, namely small areas of grass; the park has half-hidden restaurants and snack-bars catering for a tradi-tional Chinese taste of another sort. At the opposite end of the sprawling city, the Temple of the Compass gives a panorama reaching to real cliffs and hollows in the distance; climbing the five hundred steps gives the Sunday excursionist and his girl friend transmigrational merit in proportion to their transpi-rational effort. For the Taiwanese young, at school or at work, there are expeditions into the magnificent local scenery, individually for the day or collectively to camp, and in summer to the beaches, which during my visit in 1979 were cold and storm-beaten but in July thirty years earlier were already attracting Chinese swimmers.

Outdoor recreation has caught on noisily in Singapore and Hong Kong; of the two, for all its densely-packed city districts, Hong Kong has the bigger expanse of open country behind its indented granite coastline. At the monastery of the Precious

Lotus, whose little chapels among the ginger flowers two thousand feet up on a remote island used to be the haunt of hardy hikers, you overnighted on one straw mat and two plates of vegetarian beancurd, until at dawn a booming gong announced the day's first *na-moh* of the litany; nowadays the monastery brings the trippers up by motor bus, on a package excursion-with-worship, to a gaudy new concrete cathedral dispensing beancurd all day long to queues at a cafeteria. There are corners of the New Territories which even ten years ago were paddy fields of exquisite charm but now are abandoned as not worth the toil when yesteryear's tillers can open a take-away at the Gorbals or the Isle of Dogs; a few abandoned valleys have been built over, but others have been turned into nature reserves and picnic parks from which all motorcars are banned. The efforts of the Hong Kong Government in my day to ban the newly-invented transistor from the footpaths on the Kowloon hills seem to have failed, but that is not surprising, for tolerance of noise – nay, loneliness without it – has been a Chinese characteristic for a very long time, and even in the new invention's earliest days, when the valleys were still put to paddy, ploughmen and women in curtained boaters already tied little sets to their plough handles. The popularity of swimming, which is universal nowadays whereas it was a novelty thirty years ago, will have spread to the mainland too in towns that are near a beach, at least since it was given the signal of approval when Chairman Mao had himself photographed with his head bobbing on the ripples of the Yangtse; but, without leisure to travel any distance from their workplaces, few people can be benefiting.

Given a maximum annual absence from work of four or five days at New Year, the New Socialist Men and Women of China have no scope for going away on holiday; as one can see at railway-station ticket offices, travel permits have been abolished, and there is no sign of the provincial police and customs inspectors who used cantankerously to hold up departure during the civil war; but the local limits of validity of food coupons would rule out long journeys for ordinary folk anyway. On the other hand, the holiday horizon has widened vastly for the Overseas Chinese: taste for foreign air travel is mobilizing cohorts of Chinese tourists from Bangkok and Djakarta, Medan and Pahang, alongside the older-established cohorts of Japanese behind their couriers' little flags. A bachelor friend in Hong Kong invited my wife and me to dinner at a restaurant because his Cantonese 'amah' had taken her daughter off for a week on a package tour to the Philippines; the majority of guests in Southeast Asia's international hotels are Chinese, relishing the glassed-in air-conditioning and voguish foreign delicacies meant for the Monsieur Hulots. In the torrid heat of Southeast Asia, the Overseas Chinese used to yearn for the home country in which they had been so much worse off, but were lucky to get back to once in a lifetime (though surer of it once they were dead); today, a trip to Hong Kong has become an annual treat even for industrial workers, and it is common in the lobby to overhear a dumpy grandmother in old-fashioned magyar tunic explaining in Kong-Moon Cantonese to her zoot-suited grandson, who answers back disrespectfully in Malay or Thai, what was where in the days before she emigrated to marry grandfather. Ever since 1949, there has been a trickle of traffic of Overseas Chinese visiting close relatives in their home villages in South China, but not many outright holidaymakers are venturing as far as Peking yet; the hesitation is not because they might be kept there – as they would have been during the Cultural Revolution – but because their government overseas might look askance at their passports when they got back.

Social concern for workers' welfare is an idea imported into the Chinese world with the industrial techniques that call for it, and it is still nothing like so deepseated as it is in its original home in the West. In Malaya during one of the many crises of the rubber industry, a few months before the outbreak of the Korean War brought the world rubber depression to an end, it fell to me to propose to groups of tappers a contract with their employers, under which their pay – which had been tied directly to the mercurial price for the product on world markets – would be cushioned against slumps but also not soar in the booms. Generally speaking, the Indian tappers were keen on it, but the Chinese almost to a man turned the idea down, preferring to extract the maximum from the market for their labour when the price was high and take their chance when it went down. It is not surprising, given this social philosophy, that trade unions have not arisen spontaneously in the Chinese world, in or out of China itself. In part, among the Overseas Chinese, the lack of unions can be explained by the entrenched position of more traditional guilds;[3] behind the guilds there used to lurk the hand of secret societies, whose members long ago included both employers and immigrant coolies and which preyed on the labour market as one of several mutually-supporting mafia activities. Street battles were fought in Singapore and in Perak, before and after the Second World War, between secret societies aligned in China's politics with Chiang Kai-shek and unions sponsored by the Malayan Communist Party – which regarded itself as a section of Mao Tsê-tung's Party – for or against strikes and hartals in which intimidated labourers provided the riot-fodder. In this environment, trade unions, where they do exist in Chinese communities, owe their existence chiefly to governments; although, despite that, they have proved anything but subservient to the governments of Hong Kong, Singapore and Malaysia, and in those places have gained notable improvements in conditions of work and pay on their own initiative, with periodical recourse to strikes, they have been prevented, there and elsewhere, from mobilizing their industrial power for political aims beyond the immediate interests of their members.

In Taiwan and in the People's Republic, as in other People's Democracies trade unions are an arm of the ruling Party, covering in Taiwan barely a fifth of the labour force. They concern themselves with members' welfare at work, and in Taiwan act as friendly societies offering investment-based insurance, but they have no part in the strikes which occasionally occur under both governments. On the mainland, trade unions have a closed-shop status in the same way as do other 'mass movements' under Party management, such as youth, women's and peasants' associations (to one or other of which everybody is required to belong). But even that negligible liberty was taken away under Mao Tsê-tung in 1966, and the unions were dissolved; after 1973 their place was taken by 'assemblies of workers' representatives', and more recently there has reappeared on the industrial scene an 'All-China

Federation of Trade Unions'. (The new body will probably seek international contacts.) Subscriptions are obligatory but very low; in exchange members receive little perquisites like haircuts.

It is logical that, under a system where the worker's labour is owned collectively rather than by himself, he should not be free to move from one employment to another according to his own wish but should work where he is directed to. Marxians commonly argue that, because workers are 'objectively wage slaves' under capitalism, they are actually freer under direction of labour by the Party; yet the evidence is that peasants enrolled in communes are tied permanently to their land, whereas in the days of private tenure, if the opportunity of another livelihood did crop up, they could sell their holding and take it. Numbers of peasants who migrated from their communes in the 1970s to work in state factories in nearby towns were summoned sternly in 1979 to return to the land, not merely to collect their ration coupons as in the recent past, but to do their share of the dirty jobs again. In so far as the social structure of the Chinese countryside before Liberation is classed by the Marxists as 'feudal' simply because it was in a 'pre-capitalist stage of development', it did not in fact exhibit the characteristics of true feudalism at that time – indeed, unlike Japan, China had not been feudal for a thousand years, if ever; but, had the peasant's present relationship to the land and commune, and his lack of relationship to any branch of government except through the commune, been defined in terms of a law, that law would have had to read very like a prescription for serfdom. Not only is the worker not free to choose his employment, but, by the same logic, he has no absolute right to his wages, which are liable to be mulcted by way of punishment, as one instance proves, of a 'child fee' for political misdemeanours such as begetting a fourth child contrary to the current Party line. When there was a strike for more money a few months ago at a dumpling-soup factory in Shanghai, the leader was dismissed and three of his supporters forced to reimburse out of their pay the cost of the uncooked food that had gone bad.

'Back-to-the-land' was presumably enforced in 1979 as a remedy for the unemployment in the towns, which had risen to the order of twenty million workers – officially half a million in Peking alone at the end of 1976. Under the Constitution, it is contrary to socialism to pay men except for work done; but, even without that ideological explanation, the truth is that Convention No. 102 of the International Labour Organization, in so far as it calls for unemployment benefit, is all but a dead letter throughout the Chinese world, and any benefits a worker may have the right to must come from an employer, not from the state – workmen's compensation, severance pay and so on. (Taiwan has a national contributory insurance scheme which includes a 'dole', but, although it is supposed to be compulsory, it is admitted that only one worker in three actually does belong.) Similarly, no retired Chinese workers in the private sector anywhere can draw a state pension, although, in the early 1950s, we took a step in that direction in Malaya and in Singapore by setting up statutory national provident funds under which every worker, and every employer on behalf of every worker, had and has to contribute to a nest-egg encashable at any time for house purchase, but otherwise only on retirement (aged 55); under the management of trustees, I found in 1979 that the two funds have prospered spectacularly, giving the entire work force a vested interest in capitalism through, for example, the financing of property development for the expanding economy, the rents of which are credited to workers' deposits. In Hong Kong there is no such fund, but a number of employers operate schemes privately under government inspection, giving the employee the right to take the balance with him when he leaves the employment. In Taiwan, foreign and the better Chinese employers pay a gratuity on retirement after long service, but no pension.

Traditionally, Chinese people worked till they could not, and then families looked after them – in recent times, lineages; in the People's Republic, working members of the family nowadays are hard put to it to support the elderly even under circumstances where family ties are not weakening, and the concept of a state pension is confined to grace-and-favour compensation for victims of persecution in former Maoist purges who are now too old to earn their living; there is no national contributory scheme for ordinary men and women. In the last year or two, there has been talk of introducing non-contributory pensions for peasants, as a charge on the other members of the commune who are still working. New China News Agency has stated that, in the region of the capital, as many as ten thousand retired workers, over the age of sixty-five for men and fifty-five for women, have already been allotted pensions since 1977, the amounts ranging from fourteen to twenty-six dollars a month. On one of the communes, peasants were allotted half the annual average workpoints for the previous twenty years – *if*, one may hazard, the records had survived the Cultural Revolution – and that was supposed to be yielding 250 dollars a year for the men and 150 dollars for the women. On my visit to Shanghai, I asked the manager at Hsin Ching about pensions. Yes, he replied, women received one at age sixty, men at sixty-five, and the amount comes to a third of current average earnings on the commune – or rather (under pressure from me), the scheme will be going into effect soon, in five out of the nine production brigades into which the members of the labour force are divided. I asked *him* about records – especially what would happen if a peasant were transferred from one brigade to another that did not give pensions; but there was no answer.

Safety and welfare of workers has become part of the public philosophy in Southeast Asia, in Hong Kong, and in Taiwan, in small degree in consequence of the inner conviction of the authorities in those places, but much more definitely because of their exposure to the view of a foreign press capable of getting their markets in Europe or America or Australia cut off, on the grounds of unfair competition for the corresponding industries in those countries, all of which have very active trade-union movements. For example, during one of the years when I was handling public relations in the Hong Kong Government (1958), a fifth of all the women's undergarments sold in drapers' shops in the USA were said to have been manufactured in Hong Kong; as soon as that fact came to light, we had an extra-vigorous drive in the government to get factory conditions improved to a level that would satisfy reasonable critics. The government in Taiwan has shown similar sensitivity to world opinion – with an eye particularly to comparisons with Japan – and it is fair to say that pressure of foreign public opinion has been one of the less-known benefits of the economic miracle on our side of the bamboo curtain. But on the other side of it, there is no world-market factor at work to humanize a socialist transformation operating in the interests of dictatorship-of-the-proletariat-under-Party-management: there are neither factory acts nor factory inspectors in China, and, at best, one shopfloor worker is assigned by the Party activist of the establishment to keep an eye on possible hazards, as one of his or her unpaid *political* duties additional to demands of the work-bench. I did not visit big industrial plants, but the silk mill which my group was allowed into had no proper ventilation for the steam, the furniture factory had no heating against the cold of the winter weather we were all shivering in – and twenty per cent absenteeism from illness was marked up on the performance board; not only were the lavatories noisome, but in the workplaces where workers were not actually wearing all the clothes they had brought with them, garments were hanging over chairs or on improvised hooks, with no improvement on the conditions under which those undertakings were originally opened in pre-Liberation – indeed, pre-Japanese occupation – days. A conference had just been announced to discuss safety in the mines, probably called for by the number of serious accidents, of which the T'angshan earthquake disaster in 1975 is believed by China-watchers to have brought to light grave deficiencies in working methods and rescue facilities; in contemporary China, these things are left to the total discretion of a Party manager on his toes to boost productivity lest he be charged with lack of revolutionary ardour. On the other hand, it is not only in People's China that, unless there is strict enforcement of rules, factory workers are often twice bitten before they are once shy.

What if a Chinese worker does have an accident or is ill? There are no national health services anywhere in the Far East yet, even in socialist China, although anybody who can get to a hospital can usually expect the medical or surgical part of the treatment free; nursing and food have to be either paid for or provided by the patient's family. It is equally true to say that the number of hospital beds has grown enormously in the past thirty years; but there generalization about the two sides of the bamboo curtain ceases. The number of new beds provided in government hospitals in Singapore, Hong Kong and Taiwan has brought all those places up to the best international standards; patients are usually means-tested, but a proportion in Singapore, Malaysia and Hong Kong get treatment and beds free, either from the taxpayer or, as in Taiwan, from the widespread medical insurance schemes provided by employers and, if more rarely, by workers themselves out of their rising wages. The compactness of the territories that have to be catered for makes provision of rural health services comparatively simple, and their provision at employers' expense has been a statutory requirement on tin mines and on rubber estates in Malaysia (the biggest rural Chinese industries) for more than half a century. Whereas standards of medical and surgical practice have been rising constantly in the outside world since 1949 and have been passed on as a developmental by-product of world trade by external examination in the medical schools outside China, the increasing isolation fostered by Mao Tsê-tung in his last years, though never stultifying progress in the People's Republic altogether – for example, in micro-surgery to regraft severed limbs, which has been taught to, not learnt from, the outside world – delayed its extension to the benefit of the masses as a whole, most notably by suspending proper medical training during the years of the Cultural Revolution.

At Hsin Ching they had their own little hospital; most of the patients were there for acupuncture, but one man and one woman had had major surgical operations and were recovering with saline drips. We did not enter the theatre, which was said to be in use, but the neglect of hygiene and of antisepsis was plain to the eye – in the very suburbs of Shanghai; of the nearly two million hospital beds comprising the national stock according to official figures, the majority must be in institutions of this kind. Some patients got transferred, it was said, to a bigger hospital in the city; a member of our group took her sprained ankle there and found the casualty ward to be a model of cleanliness. On the commune, the service is financed by a levy on workers' annual emoluments, but for services at a distance I was told (and it has been mentioned in the Party press from time to time) a fee would be charged, of which the patient would pay a fifth and the commune four-fifths. Far from the city, it appears, there are only barefoot doctors, who have had six months' training of sorts and combine medical duties with tractor-servicing or muck-spreading; the Party in Hainan published a reminder the year before my visit that not

fewer than 120 days' non-medical work must be done by the
'auxiliary doctors' in a year. The barefooter's stock-in-trade is
herbal medicine, of which the peasant old wives must feel they
have as good a command as he. One knows from Party
condemnations of it that peasants still prefer to have recourse
to the cures of spirit mediums, ignoring Party propaganda.
On the medical front, therefore, there will have been
improvement in the quality of life since Liberation, but
rather more for the Chinese people who have not been liberated.

The Chinese temperament is as provident as it is industrious,
and the little deposit-and-loan banks that are so prominent in
small-town life in the USA have been so in the Chinese world
for even longer, but closely tied to buying and selling gold: the
first hijacking of an aircraft that ever took place in the world
was that of a flying-boat taking off from Macau for Hong
Kong in 1948 with an illicit consignment of the metal, as a
hedge in the civil war: three Pearl-River pirates who had
bought tickets evidently tried to overpower the crew as if the
plane were a tow-boat – at the cost of all the lives on board
except one of their own. The gold shops in Southeast Asia and
Taiwan, and the money-shops in Hong Kong, still trade very
largely, as they did thirty years ago, on workers' savings,
accepting short-term deposits of cash at interest and making
longer-term loans at a higher rate – a speculative business
close to the margins of the gambling that is another element in
the national temperament. Surprisingly, though gold shops
are certainly not tolerated any more, there is provision for
workers to invest their little savings in the socialist economy of
the People's Republic as well. Even before Liberation, it was
only a very sophisticated segment of Chinese society that held
private current accounts with banks, and there has been no
occasion to introduce them under the communist regime; but
private deposit accounts do exist in the town branches of state
banks, paying an interest of barely half one per cent a year and
lending back, sometimes with supplements from state funds,
for development of the savers' collectives at rates of three to
five per cent. The amount of such deposits is not likely to be
divulged in official statistics until the regime has taken bigger

strides in candour than so far, but the very existence of private accounts proves that not all workers are held to subsistence level in their standard of living. The interest is low, but depositors are shielded from the twin risks of inflation and bank-crashes which were notorious under the old regime – and which hit small savers in Hong Kong again five or six years ago; some of them must hope that when the state eventually withers away in fulfilment of Engels's prediction, state banks will somehow not wilt with it. Meanwhile, ironically, banks have turned out to be as great a lure to the armed robber in People's China as banks in capitalist countries, and several raiders who committed murder in hold-ups have been executed in recent years.

For Marxist – Leninists, the 'toiling class' includes not only industrial workers and peasants but also soldiers, both as targets for subversion and sedition before the revolution is complete and afterwards, when the communist party has become the government. In many parts of the world, military service is a burdensome interruption to the worker's vocational career; that is true for some young Chinese today. In past ages, besides local militias for security against bandits, the stronger dynasties in China maintained an imperial guard and a corps of military mandarins who were regularly entrusted with civil and magisterial duties in frontier provinces. On the whole, however, soldiers were rather a despised class, and until this century neither the discipline nor the dangers of soldiering impinged much on the masses' lives. Before Liberation, there was no law enforcing compulsory military service, and the 'volunteers' I observed in 1948 from my tow-boat being hauled off to Manchuria for the civil war had been press-ganged. There used in those days to be a widespread idea among Europeans in Southeast Asia that young Chinese had an aversion to wearing uniforms; the fact is that they got little chance under colonial regimes, which treated them as temporary residents and 'unsuitable' even as police. Today, they join the police in Macau and Hong Kong but could not very well be trained as soldiers, with guns facing towards China. In Indonesia, the one-time colonial objection to Chinese recruits to the army is stronger today than thirty years ago; it also applies in Thailand, Burma and the Philippines. There has been a handful of Overseas Chinese in the moss-trooping bands of Cambodia, but the two Chinese generals who helped the Vietnamese Communists to power were disgraced in 1978 for the 'colonial' reason. The present-day Malaysian army is for all races but wholly volunteer; Chinese youths do not join up in practice. Singapore is a complete contrast, for Chinese conscription for national service is regarded as a means of racial integration and 'nation-building'; a recent survey of attitudes commissioned by the Singapore Government reported that, on the whole, the short-term Chinese conscripts regarded their experience as unpleasant but useful, both vocationally (learning new money-earning skills) and, some of them admitted, in forming their characters.[4] Taiwan has both conscription and a standing army half a million strong that owes nothing to Chinese tradition but has been shaped on German, Russian and American models; it is technically up to date, standing-to out of sight, and soldiers go on leave in mufti – a policy opposite to that of the Communist mainland.

Indeed, one of the visual changes in People's China today, by comparison with the war period, is the presence on all sides of military uniforms – loose-fitting and conspicuous for the absence of badges of rank (warlord armies looked the same), although one can tell an officer by the four pockets on his tunic instead of the two that suffice for other ranks. (I watched to see whether men with two pockets saluted the ones with four; they did not.) Many seats in trains and aeroplanes were occupied by men in uniform – two-pocketed in trains, four-pocketed in planes. Some of the uniforms may have belonged to the militia, in which everybody has to learn to shoot unless precluded by 'unsuitable class background', but the majority were members of the standing army, promoted from the masses' organizations. Cleaner-looking than their predecessors a generation ago, but still untidy by foreign standards, they mingled with the crowds in the streets, in twos and threes, or at the Zoo, in the palaces and museums, and snapped each other on the turrets of the Great Wall. The psychology behind their ubiquity may well be a Party policy to emphasize that this one-time guerrilla force, whose generals were the Party's leaders, is still a buttress in socialist society, identified with the people's lives – especially their day-off lives, when they are out of sight of their workplace cadres. It was not difficult to understand that this force had been one of the chief actors in the political struggle of ten years ago.

4 'Boiling Small Fish'

'Dictatorship is rule based on force and unrestrained by laws'

(Lenin)

Continuously since it was first unified, before Hannibal had crossed the Alps, China has been the biggest political unit in the world; never in history has any other state comprised more than a quarter of China's population, still today uncounted by census but officially estimated to be a thousand million, of whom eight hundred million count as peasants. It follows that no precedents from the experience of other states can be urged on, or applied by, China's rulers with confidence, and when historians or political scientists criticize either the present regime or its forerunners, it behoves them to bear in mind how hard put to it any of us would be to devise alternatives that would work or that would have worked.

A Taoist contemporary of Hannibal coined a maxim for Chinese rulers (he knew of no others) that has become one of the most repeated sayings in the language: 'Governing big states must no more be overdone than boiling small fish'. The maxim in fact made a virtue out of necessity, for China's growth in area and population has always outstripped progress in communications – both the physical means of transmitting messages and the intangible area of relations between institutions, of procedures, and of the language in which to convey information and commands. The style and policy of any government is inevitably a combination of tradition (political culture), of ideas ('ideology'), and of force of circumstances – in the case of 'progressive' governments seeking above all an extension of their power, one can say of opportunity. In not a few of the policies in contemporary China commended to the masses by the Party as revolutionary

innovations, it is possible, paradoxically, to discern continuity
with the old regime whose shortcomings, in standard Marxian
argument, the Party criticizes in exaggerated terms in order to
justify its own revolutionary excesses. When I first went there
in the late 1940s, Chiang Kai-shek had just decreed a liberal
constitution, promising the people a brave post-war world of
modernized administration from the restored capital at
Nanking; a few reforms had been inaugurated a dozen years
earlier, only to be frustrated by the civil war and the Japanese
invasion. Now Chiang was being kept out of Manchuria by
Stalin and Truman until Mao Tsê-tung had control of it, and
he had barely taken back the foreign concessions surrendered
by Japan after its defeat and reasserted China's sovereignty
(against Stalin's encroachments) over Turkestan; he had not
progressed even that far in Tibet, still less had time to legislate
for administration in any of the repossessed provinces. Mao,
by restarting the civil war from Manchuria, made sure he
never did. The greater efficiency, by common consent, of
governments manned by Chinese personnel outside China
today has been facilitated, in not a few of the instances noted in
chapter 3, by the smaller territory and population for which
those governments have been responsible.

From the peasant's point of view, government in China
(though dictatorial at the centre) has always been indirect for
want of direct links between subject and state. An important
example is the field of taxation: no individual in China has
ever paid income tax, in imperial times or since, and tax on the
immense rural areas has always been assessed and, with few
exceptions in history, collected by districts or, now, by
'collective collection' through communes.[1] Apportionment
among individuals in the past was a matter, not of state
fairness, but of bargaining among neighbours (in lineages,
cousins). Although today's nationwide tax rate on collectives is
alleged not to absorb more than three and a half per cent of
the product, targets for tax yield are fixed at five-year intervals
in advance – save for the actual number of years, on time-
honoured principle. The system cannot take account adminis-
tratively of real income for retrospective assessment, and
consequently, except perhaps vaguely in state enterprises, the
idea of personal contribution through taxes to the cost of
defence and other government responsibilities is never borne

in on workers' minds. In collectives, and especially communes, tax is a first charge on the gross annual accounts, and only after that and various second charges have been met can income be distributed, as a third charge, according to individual workpoints; the value of workpoints is fixed locally by dividing the total number having to be honoured by the commune into the surplus balance available after meeting the prior charges – a little like a dividend on shares, except that what has been invested is labour and not money. (In the earlier stages of collectivization, before the 'highest stage' of the commune was inaugurated, a dividend was also allotted according to the individual member's investment of land, farm animals, or tools, in addition to what he was paid on workpoints; but that ceased to be the practice from about 1958.) Personal circumstances do not come into taxation, and work groups have been making sure lately of their own share first, then telling the accountants higher up the commune that they have nothing left to pay any contribution to the gross tax demanded by the authorities. Since in practice the tax seems to be paid largely in kind, at the same time as consignments of 'state purchases' – levied over and above, in quantities and at prices fixed by the government, in a manner indistinguishable from tax in the eyes of the cultivators, one must suppose – there is some resemblance here as well to the imperial practice of referring to tax as 'tribute' and moving it round the country in convoys of waggons or barges. The imperial policy of abating the burden of tribute as a political concession to recalcitrant regions also survives today, for example in the recent suspension of all levies for tax and procurement in Tibet.

    In Southeast Asia and the non-communist Chinese territories also, direct personal taxation makes a minor contribution to government budgets. Income taxes exist in these places, but other sources of finance from the boom economies make either their extension to all categories of wage-earners, or their imposition at rates comparable with Western countries, not worth the anticipated unpopularity. In Taiwan, I was told, it is common for employers to pay the tax-bills their workers receive. In no instance, however, does the neglect of direct levies result from administrative inability to impose them if the need were to arise, whereas that is the position on the mainland. It may be doubted whether, psychologically speaking, there can be representation without taxation, and it is only in Singapore, where direct taxation is at its most vigorous – whether by coincidence or by connection – that government is noticeably viewed by the Chinese masses as an entity to which their own personal destinies are tied. Everywhere else, it seemed to me that government is still of interest to the public only for particular services it has to offer and for the regulations it lays down for daily life – as a distant and alien authority; from choice, government and its works are avoided.

It is a commonplace to write that the same attitude of the Chinese people to government is met with in the past, and there is copious testimony that the agents of the government shared it: they took a detached, paternal view of the relationship of governors to governed which in the twentieth century is deemed a development of colonial rule. Here is an illustration of the relationship, written from the government side about the time of William the Conqueror, by Ou-yang Hsiu of the Sung dynasty – both model and exponent of Confucian ethics:

> It was the year after your obedient servant took charge of this Ch'u district, and summertime, when I first tasted a local water of wonderful sweetness. I asked the natives where they got it from, and they showed me a place not far outside the south gate. Above, a crag, auspiciously called Hill of Plenty, rose high and sheer; below, a deep gully wound down beneath a tangle of undergrowth; and there between the two, a clear fountain bubbled up and spilled over to make a pool. It was a pretty spot with lovely views all round. I decided to excavate some of the rock and extend the pool, level the ground and make a site for a pavilion, where I myself, and the people, could come for re-creation.
>
> Early in the late wars, Ch'u district became a battlefield when the Chou forces overtook Li Ching's 150,000-strong army and routed them, capturing their two generals at the very gates of Ch'u. I like to combine my own tours of the

district with a study of its written records, and once I climbed to the top of the range to survey the passes and try to identify the spot where the vanquished were over-whelmed. But there were no longer even old folk who remembered, for so long has there been peace here. When the T'ang dynasty fell, rebellion rent the land, and brigands and petty tyrants fought among themselves over their private domains. But the Sung dynasty reunited the country and dismantled their fortresses; and now, a hundred years later, the same pure streams flow down from the same mountains, but nobody remembers that once this wilderness saw so much bloodshed.

In modern times, here between the Yangtze and the Huai, Ch'u lies off the routes of merchants and traders, unvisited by their barges and their waggons. Travellers from afar do not journey this way, and the people's life is untouched by events in the world outside; the tranquil tillage of their fields, the clothes they make themselves, the food they grow and eat – these are enough to nourish and entertain the living and provide obsequies for the dead. How could such folk appreciate by themselves what they owe to their century of peace under a just and enlightened rule?

As soon as I took over this district, I was delighted by its rustic scenes and my own uncomplicated duties, and charmed by the unpolished and unpunctual manners of the place. Once I had discovered the spring between the hill and the valley, I began to pass whole days there among the local people, gazing at the crag above and listening to the brook below. Every season offers its own delight: the sweet herbs that grow in the stony crevices, the cool shade of the noble trees – to be followed by gales and frost, ice and snow, and then the crystal dew again and the riot of spring colours.

This year the people have had an exceptional harvest and big increase of their livestock, so they can afford the time to come with me on my excursions. I point out to them how favoured they are by their landscape and their quality of life and how they enjoy the fruits of their toil because they have good government. Thus I have discharged two duties of my office – to impress on the people the virtues of Sung rule and to associate myself with the enjoyment it assures them. I have had a flowery board put up as a reminder, inscribed: 'Era of Plenty Pavilion'.

That little essay belongs to a whole genre of idylls about rustic retreats that brought Confucian officials into arm's-length touch with the masses, so to speak; by reason of the very fact that the Communist Party is 'the vanguard of the working class', it distances itself from the masses, even if it lives among them 'like fish in water' (another ancient adage). As long ago as 1948, one of my teachers, taking a China-coast view of impending events, asserted that 'Liberation' was not only a reaction, negatively, against Chiang Kai-shek's modernizing capitalism, but, positively, a restoration in some ways of imperial values, notably in what he had heard of the government of the Red Areas as a return to control through a 'moral influence' that made 'new men' of the people. Had I known more at the time, I could have pointed out that Chiang too, in the 1930s, had claimed a moral mandate to shape 'new men'; the fact is that the idea is a perennial one in China: a successor of Ou-yang Hsiu declared that ' "cherish the people" in the works of Confucius ought to be emended to "make the people new" ' – which was a Chinese play on two words written with similar characters (*ch'in min* and *hsin min*).

In fact, many coincidences of thought can be found between Confucianism and Marxism–Leninism, starting with Engels's understanding of the state as having no function but as a repressive and coercive apparatus in the hands of a partisan interest; that view was foreshadowed by another contemporary of Hannibal, Han Fei, much honoured in Mao Tsê-tung's circle. Like Sun Yat-sen's and Chiang Kai-shek's, Mao's early reading included the philosophy of the mandarin Wang Yang-ming, who lived in Henry VIII's time; his argument, concerned like all Confucianism with society rather than with individuals, and influenced by his experience of public administration, started from the proposition that there are no facts in nature (especially politics and history) but deeds, and no knowledge of them separable from participation in them. The same idea, added to by the concept of class, must have seemed to Mao to underlie Marx's 'praxis' – hence his own piece of philosophy, 'On Practice'. The opportunistic implications of the idea cannot have escaped him, summed up by his Vietnamese collaborator, Ho Chi Minh, in the aphorism, 'Truth is whatever suits the aims of the state'.

References to tradition still spring to the tongue of Chinese people of every class, no doubt prompted in part by the changelessness of their ideographic, non-phonetic writing from generation to generation, and in part by a conception of history in which there are no numerical dates, for the record of China's past is arranged comprehensively by reigns and dynasties – over shorter periods in sixty-year cycles (not centuries) – and the years in both arrangements are designated by names, not numbers. The relative antiquity of Chinese events has to be worked out every time they are mentioned – it is not self-evident to ear or eye – and in most discussion of the past it has no part. As a result, although every Chinese schoolboy knows that T'ang came before Ming, Chinese history lacks the built-in chronology implicit in saying 'eighth century', 'twelfth century', 'sixteenth century'. Progress does not find a place in the Chinese philosophy of history. The saying about not overboiling the fish has appeared in the folklore of every generation in Chinese history, and the policy of decentralized public administration accompanied by authoritarian morality has been taken for granted in all ages: Mao did not invent it.

However, it is in accordance with the Marxian standpoint (that control of the means of production is the key to politics) that the instrument of social control over the greater part of the uncentralized People's Republic should be the commune. The commune is organized primarily to manage the production of food, secondarily to manage the production of other necessities for the food producers, and only in third place as an agent of public administration. There is a break with tradition here only in the order of priorities, for in the earliest imperial times it was already a duty of government, not exactly to manage food production, but to try to influence markets so as to level out the effects of dearth and abundance – to do so by stocking-up granaries in good times and selling off in bad; the fundamental laws of economics were understood in China a thousand years before they were thought about in Europe. It is to workplaces, and especially to the rural communes, that have been assigned all duties of government, on the principle of self-determination and self-administration. As in other parts of the world where 'self-determination' has been urged in modern times, the key question is who constitutes the 'self': 'national' self-determination for an African colony has frequently ended in transfer of power to one tribe or one religious faction or an army, and under Marxist auspices the self in self-determination of the working class is always the Communist Party, its 'vanguard'.

At lower social levels in China, the self in the communes is sometimes the whole commune, sometimes the so-called production brigades (which numbered eleven at Hsin Ching), sometimes the production teams (sixty-eight) that make up the brigades, according to which of these collectivities notionally 'owns' what part of 'the means of production'. Teams and brigades are not so much subdivisions of the commune as built up from earlier stages in the process of collectivizing land and farm equipment. They represent levels in the socialist transformation of the people to make them ever more collaborative, until the last traces of individuality were meant to disappear in the communal living and feeding the regime enjoined (by persuasion-with-coercion) in the late 1950s but had to rescind, not only because its unpopularity straightaway cut down peasant willingness to work, but also because the pattern of the existing housing stock in the villages could not be physically adapted to such a way of life overnight. Today, I found, the theory is that land and hand tools belong to production teams, machinery and minor irrigation works to production brigades, major irrigation and factories – that is to say, repair shops, assembly-plants, power generators, and any 'side-line' light industries there may be enough local resources for the peasants to engage in when not working in the fields – to the whole commune; a similar gradation applies to transport, from hand-carts up to lorries. Originally, at the same time as communal living, the Party planned to raise all management to the level of the whole commune and to obliterate memories of lower-level 'ownership', presumably as a step towards 'ownership by the whole people' – that is to say, total undisguised state control. Arguments about 'the correct line' in this regard have been acrimonious, and one of the charges against Mao Tsê-tung's wife while I was on my visit was that she had used intimidation to hasten that process;

abuses had become rife, Chairman Hua was explaining, because of the inexperience of commune managers in keeping the complicated accounts. By chance, at the Dragon's Well tea estate, I came across what I take to have been an attempt to reform accountancy procedures: about a hundred men, equipped with abacuses (although pocket electronic calculators are common in China today), and said to be from various enterprises round Hangchow, were being given a lesson in book-keeping. Henceforward, came the Chairman's word over the media, the production team would be the key echelon for management (ownership and accounting), and no attempt to enlarge the units would be envisaged until an adequate reservoir of managerial talent was on hand.

It is hard to believe that, once he was expropriated under the post-revolutionary land reform, the average peasant has been much concerned over thories of ownership: he himself was no longer the owner of land, equipment or even his own labour anyway, and the details of commune management must then have been relevant to the quality of his life solely for the return he received from it in food, services or money. The government has never accepted general responsibility for social services: hospitals dispensing advanced medicine and institutes of tertiary education are managed by the state because they are useful politically to the Party, but cottage hospitals and primary schools (with much of the responsibility for secondary schools) of benefit to individuals must be provided by the people themselves on the commune, since the central government could not manage them on a nationwide scale. Similarly in the towns, members of industrial collectives have to provide their own social services, and health and education facilities are located, I believe, within the perimeters of state enterprises as well, there being no district authority that could be made to act as manager of dispensaries or elementary schools. Managerial deficiencies, compounded by technical backwardness, also explain the failure to introduce nationally-organized workmen's compensation and pension schemes; provident funds are precluded by lack of a capitalist sector in the national economy in which to invest the money put aside. When it comes to safety and factory inspection, there has been the additional consideration that the Party could not countenance an authority in the state appointed to exercise independent judgement, and therefore to compete with itself: totalitarianism is essential for the integrity of the Party's high revolutionary purpose. But it would be surprising if many Chinese people were aware of the benefits available outside China which for these various reasons they are denied.

Decentralization and totalitarianism are in logic opposed, but 'the unity of opposites' is one of those logical conundrums which help Marxists delight in their own ingenuity. The opposites are reconciled in People's China by the procedures of democratic centralism, which enables the Party to combine actual dominion over the lowliest individual with the appearance of responsiveness to the will of the masses, of which, however, it is itself the only spokesman. The centralism is 'democratic' because it does not operate by explicit command; again, I believe the reason is the size and diversity of the country. The Party draws up its 'lines' couched in slogan form; they may or may not be published before they go into effect – go into effect not by debated decision of a legislative body but by announcement in the media. The Party Politburo has a monopoly of initiation of lines; in important matters it is an open secret that the lines translate the will of the Leader – the *vozhd*, as Lenin and Stalin were called – whether blatantly as in the days of Mao or more modestly as in those of Têng and Hua. The most important lines will be submitted to a 'plenum' of the Party's Central Committee, and, when a really radical change of policy or a wide-ranging concentration of manpower is entailed, a full Party Congress may be convened to endorse it. Whatever its significance on this scale of importance, the line has to be discussed and approved (without option to disapprove) at lower echelons of the Party and, finally – in a 'democratic' extension of democratic centralism beyond the ranks of the Party alone – at meetings of members of the collectives and communes, at which attendance is compulsory and the proceedings are guided by a cadre to the correct conclusion. In many instances, the core of the agenda is simply how to implement the new line in detail in regard to the management of the collective, but, in any case, the implications of the policy are brought home to even the least intelligent, potential objections can be rebutted in advance by arguments which, if not always credible, are bowed to as authoritative, and the Leader back in Peking is assured of the unanimous collective approval of the nation for what he has decreed, not only in matters economic, but in every aspect of social and political life from family planning to the Sino-Soviet dispute. All these matters fall within the orbit of workplaces in the decentralized collective system of government. The proportion of the worker's time that has been wasted on political meetings has become notorious abroad and is believed to have amounted sometimes to a quarter of the working day; I asked at the Dragon's Well whether that was still true and, to my surprise, got the reply that it had been in the past, but nowadays not more than an hour or two a month goes on such 'activity'. At Hsin Ching, an ex-Polish communist on our tour asked the chief guide how the Party applied the managerial sagacity he was extolling to make sure of unanimous endorsements; the question was political, she was told, and therefore improper from a tourist.

One of the hardest things to find out in China is the degree of private reserve with which the masses conform to the system. In my river towboat days, the Chinese I encountered were talkative – downright garrulous – with foreigners; this time, the serene expressions on their faces were uniformly equable as their suits were uniformly blue, but they were taciturn: in the north, my Peking dialect might be to blame, but when I did strike up a conversation with the Canton crowd, they chatted only until a large figure pushed his way in, and then they melted away. To what extent do the masses really believe that the interests of the collectivity to which they belong – never by personal choice – and which is their contact with the government and Party mean more for the quality of their life than their individual interests do? Or, put the way that Party pronouncements usually prefer, do they really believe the collective interest is identical with their own? – as they would presumably believe if socialist transformation had made New Men of them. In some respects, the question resembles the one posed in Western countries by closed-shop trade unionism and collective bargaining; but in China it is rendered more acute by the fact that the worker is not allowed to change his employment and that the collectivity embraces his whole life – even sometimes directing his choice of a spouse. It is true that a variety of arrangements for collectivized ownership and cultivation of the arable land, and in certain respects communal (lineage) living, has been widespread in China's past: Ou-yang Hsiu was instrumental in institutionalizing the single-lineage village based on such arrangements, with the furtherance of social control and security of the regime, under conditions of decentralization, consciously in mind. At that time too the head of lineage or village had the power to prescribe marriage alliances, and there are many communist stories of 'rich peasants' (usually lineage chiefs) in modern, but pre-Liberation, times who lorded it over poor peasants (or relations) just as totally – including the choice of a spouse – but for selfish reasons lacking the rationalizations advanced today; for the like of poor peasants in those stories there is a modicum of change in the quality of life and probably for the better.

The Marxist–Leninist reordering of Chinese society is therefore not all that innovatory, and passivity towards the authorities and avoidance of confrontation with them, already marked in imperial times and under Chiang Kai-shek and observable in Southeast Asian countries today where the Chinese are minorities, are habits that have on the whole changed little. None the less, the Party has evidently had cause to be apprehensive about worker resistance, and here a true innovation has been made: the system of criticism and self-criticism meetings at regular intervals, reserved in European communist countries as a kind of confessional for maintenance of inner Party discipline, has been extended in China, like the political meetings, to ordinary workers of the non-Party sector as well; doubtless in many places the two kinds of meeting have become mixed up. Everybody has to own up to some error on his part in order to justify picking holes in other people, and in the general cross-accusations the Party cadre in charge needs no exceptional shrewdness to spot undercurrents and forestall organized opposition. Individuals nevertheless are foolhardy enough to speak out on occasion against the system, and in cases where it proves insufficient to 'struggle' them by turning their workmates against them under penalty of risking the label 'counter-revolutionary' themselves, banishment for manual labour at a distance from home has been common, and for indefinite periods, until some other Party cadre shows clemency by pronouncing the culprit 're-educated' – that is to say, until his spirit has been broken.

It is sometimes asserted in the West that the slight regard for law and justice shown in China since Liberation is no more than traditional political culture – that law was purely repressive in the past, that it conferred no rights on the subject or citizen, and that it was rarely enforced strictly but served simply as a guide for administrative action by the mandarins of the territorial administration, who doubled as magistrates in the same way as district commissioners did in Western colonial dependencies. All of that is broadly true, but the faults in concepts of law and justice in imperial times should not be exaggerated: undoubtedly they were affected by the geographical factor, as was the administration, and by the desire of mandarins like Ou-yang Hsiu to exert benign influence rather than to meticulously apply rules; but the emperor's subjects benefited, if not from defined and enforceable 'human rights', at least from a system of ethics which laid on the ruler and his agents moral duties of fairness, clemency and incorruptibility. Although the traditional system was precise about the duties of underlings to serve superiors but vaguer in its injunctions of benevolence for superiors' treatment of underlings, and imperial history recorded innumerable examples of back-sliding by superiors even from those vague injunctions, the guilty men were sternly condemned and severely punished. 'Revolutionary morality' lays no duties on the authorities, and the citizen has no greater protection from the ethical system than from the legal: both embody only his duties to the state – and through the state to the Party.

The defects of the imperial courts in Western eyes were a stick with which to beat China in the Unequal Treaties of the nineteenth century and to demand extra-territoriality; Chinese intellectuals came on the whole to agree with the criticisms, however, and, bent on restoring national self-esteem, began to study European and American law, its philosophy and practice, for themselves. Warlords and power struggles slowed but did not halt progress down to 1949 in bringing China's law and justice in the main cities into line with prevailing international standards and in training judges and private lawyers; but the reforms did not penetrate deep into Chinese society or far into the interior. In a hundred contexts under Kuomintang rule, although China's intellectuals may in private have recognized the need for strict legality in state action, the ordinary citizen in practice reaped no benefit in his daily life.

The Communist Party extended throughout the country the hierarchy of 'people's courts' – manipulated by the cadres by the same tactics as political meetings were – that had been introduced first in Red Areas during the civil war. All existing laws were repealed: criminals and deviants were reckoned counter-revolutionaries, since their behaviour was inconsistent with the socialist ideal. But the pre-Liberation courts were left in being and apparently went on handing down judgements as best they could in a gradually dwindling jurisdiction, not finally going under until the Cultural Revolution. Once the whole economy had been collectivized or nationalized under a Party management not answerable to any principle or external authority, there was no call for the codes and procedures of commercial or property law enacted barely a dozen years before. But civil disputes within the neighbourhood or family, typified in the story in Chapter 1, arise in all Chinese times and places; they are still settled by mediation, I was told in 1979, but with the difference that conciliators, whether Party members or not, must not make any arrangement inconsistent with current Party lines that might have a bearing on the matter. A customary law will probably have tended to grow up province by province to make good the lack of statutes, but there is no way of finding out. Recent denunciations of 'leading cadres' for buying agricultural land from production teams (officially recognized as 'owners' once more) and to have private houses built on it suggests that private ownership of residential land, never formally abolished by the present regime, is safeguarded in the minds of the purchasers, either by their personal unchallengeability as Party cadres, or by continued recognition of private property in the customs of the times.

From the point in law reform at which Chiang Kai-shek was halted on the mainland, Taiwan has gone forward. The Kuomintang is structurally like a communist party, for it still keeps to the constitution drafted for it by the Bolsheviks in Canton and approved by Sun Yat-sen six weeks before he died in 1925; its will prevails over law and justice in matters where the security of the regime is at stake, but even there efforts have been made, if more from foreign pressure than inner conviction, to frame security needs in statutory form and to bring cases against political dissidents in the courts, reserving detention by political direction as a last resort. Even before the Second World War, the Kuomintang had a policy of organized cooperation among smallholders, and the desirability of improving land utilization in Taiwan by reviving it was under discussion in 1979; nevertheless, the Taiwanese economy retains its determinedly capitalist shape, and that fact, as well as its dependence on international trade, makes a code of commercial law indispensable, and the jurisdiction of the courts is much as in the world at large; there are schools of law and private lawyers – all that is lacking is provision for legal aid for the poor. In Macau and in Hong Kong there exists the same range of statutory law as in Europe, and it is administered in courts where judges and lawyers are mostly Chinese; side by side with the official system, traditional mediation is recognized as the right procedure in petty civil disputes, except that the conciliators are usually Chinese members of elected local councils in Hong Kong, unofficial representatives of the Chinese Communist Party among the boatmen and factory workers of Macau. The lives of the Chinese citizens of Singapore are touched by law in much the same way as if they were in Hong Kong, except that mediation of disputes takes them into labour welfare departments of the government, for local councils are manned by political party machines, not by local notables. Unlike Hong Kong, Singapore does have detention without trial, though only for cases of revolutionary subversion; as in Taiwan, the power is on its statute book and is circumscribed by safeguards for the detainee that the government dare not overstep.

Chinese people in Malaysia are similarly placed to the Singaporeans, except that the courts and legal profession are multi-racial and the forces of law and order under non-Chinese command; they too face detention without trial if they step onto forbidden political ground, but here there are two patches – not only revolutionary subversion and aid to the communist guerrillas in the jungle, but also that of incitement to racial discontent and tension in the fast-growing towns. In Indonesia, Chinese ethnic identification with the legal and judicial apparatus is at its lowest, the area of political ground that is dangerous for them at its widest: after the failure of *Gestapu* (an acronym for 30 September) – the Indonesian Communist Party's *coup d'état* in 1965, encouraged and abetted by the Chinese People's Republic – tens of thousands of Chinese inhabitants were slaughtered and thousands confined in concentration camps for periods of up to ten or a dozen years. The Chinese in Indonesia have had no redress, and I found the fear of being rounded up a second time a dominant factor in the quality of the life of several I spoke to; in such matters, they did not expect protection from the Indonesian courts. In Thailand, Chinese people are so closely integrated with Siamese society that large numbers call themselves by Thai names; they suffer no fears of arbitrary action by authority – so long as they refrain from racial assertiveness – and in the civil and commercial affairs that are their daily concern have enjoyed here too, since the 1870s, protection of a legal and judicial system built up by the Siamese monarchy (whose own 'unequal treaties' kept the fate of China in the forefront of its attention) to standards that were meant all the time to render Thailand safe from criticism as socially backward, unfit to govern its ethnic-minority provinces on the borders of French Indochina and British Malaya, and unworthy of international recognition based on *equal* treaties.

Degrees of, and mechanisms for, what political scientists call 'participation' vary for Chinese people in different countries nowadays as widely as do the legal systems governing their lives. The Chinese in Siam are Thai citizens and belong to the same political parties as their native hosts, vote in elections, and part-own the political press. In Indonesia, five out of six Chinese are citizens and similarly can vote in elections, but even those have to be careful not to get involved in controversial public discussion that could be held against them in another Gestapu. In Malaysia the proportion of non-citizens in the Chinese community is very small, and citizens of

Chinese race enjoy equal rights to vote with members of other races, subject to limitation on public discussion, even inside the parliament chamber, only on the same two patches of contentious ground: any question touching on Malay privilege in the body politic and social is taboo. In Singapore there is universal suffrage, and it is genuinely through the ballot box that there has emerged a one-party rule, such as to rejoice the hearts of Marxist–Leninist revolutionaries, were it not dedicated to frustration of Marxist–Leninist revolution. In Taiwan, as well, there is one-party rule, for the more usual reason that the party fought its way into office at gunpoint, bringing its readymade legislature with it from the mainland thirty years ago; after twenty years a few extra representatives of Taiwan constituencies were added, but it was not until after Chiang Kai-shek died in 1975 that non-Kuomintang candidates were allowed to stand – and even they, during my visit, were in trouble for trying to form an opposition *party*. In so far as the daily lives of the people are dominated by more humdrum concerns of government, however, any aspirations to parliamentary democracy may, since 1951, have been satisfied, as the regime claims, by a provincial legislature, not competent in matters of public security, election to which is free and open. In Hong Kong, in contrast to all other communities of Chinese abroad, there is no whiff of parliamentary democracy, because colonial emancipation would run counter to vested interests, not in London, but in Peking: even if an honest electoral register could be compiled in Hong Kong, a pernicious example would be set for the People's Republic, and the measure would have to be condemned in Peking as an act of sovereignty on Britain's part calculated to arouse demands for independence of the Colony – of all possible destinies for Hong Kong, the least acceptable to whoever rules China.

In imperial China, only one parliament ever sat, at the very end, and its members were appointed by the Court; the Kuomintang ruled without a legislature until 1948, and even then had to resort to appointment because of disturbed conditions in so/many of the provinces. As a result, the communist system in no sense amounted to deprivation of rights conceded by previous regimes. Under 'democratic centralism', the 'vanguard' Party in power is a pyramid of committees (culminating in the Chairman), the members of each of which all up the scale elect the next one higher (the democracy); at the same time, the committees are invested with a reverse power of destitution of the lower by the higher (the centralism). The state apparatus, which is the answerable repository of power where the Party is the actual repository, is a similar electoral pyramid, with the electorate at the base comprising the whole adult population instead of just members of the Party. Candidates for state committees are designated by the Party, and the original 1953 electoral law (still in force) laid down 'equal-quota candidature'; that means that the number of candidates in each constituency must not exceed the number of seats and that the 'election' is not an expression of choice but of approval – in effect, compulsory approval, since difficulties can be made in other spheres of the individual's life under the same controlling hand of the Party if he 'shows a negative attitude' by absenting himself from the ballot. From the end of 1980 onwards, there is to be a reform in the system, to the extent that 'unequal quotas' will be brought in, allowing the proportion of candidates to delegates elected to be raised to three or four to two. A further reform has been mooted though not adopted, namely the extension of direct suffrage to the second echelon up the hierarchy, but the Party is specially enjoined, if that does go ahead, to retain, nay strengthen, its 'leadership' over the conduct of the new type of election.

The approbatory nature of elections is repeated in the proceedings of the bodies elected: the National People's Congress (3500 strong) rarely meets – and for several years during the Cultural Revolution went into total abeyance – any business it is very desirable for it to endorse (never initiate) being entrusted to a standing committee. Lower councils meet more frequently, but they too work (under Party direction) principally through standing committees, in which all their pseudo-powers are vested. There is also an appointed People's Political Consultative Conference (2000 strong) representing sectional interests – religious associations, trade unions, certain minorities, and until recent years (and détente with Southeast Asian governments) the Overseas Chinese – but its gatherings are rarer still, although one was being prepared during my visit; the Conference has a National

Committee and a Standing Committee of the National Committee, which both meet more often. The system makes no
provision for debates; indeed, the Great Hall of the People in
Peking (built as aid by Russian architects, and its Chinese
decoration confined to removable pictures on the walls of its
committee rooms), where sessions of the top organs take
place, including the Communist Party, could easily be adapted
as a theatre or cinema, but visibly never as a debating
chamber.

The great mass of the people in China probably do not give
much thought to whether the Communist Party's vaunted
democracy has substance; refugees' reports about low-level
political meetings, at which the 'participation' of workers and
peasants in discussion of public issues theoretically finds
expression, show that they are treated as an irksome obligation. But there can be little doubt that intellectuals have a
clearer appreciation of the implications of the make-believe
and a quite definite understanding of the meaning of the
language of politics and government used by the Party in
the countries where it originated. Few say anything about the
matter, and none would do anything, but I found that what
was at stake, by way of debunking the system, in the
development of the 'democracy walls' was grasped with great
clarity – and the possible consequences of being seen there
were consistently avoided by the guides on my tour by keeping
well away.

5 From Mandarin to Cadre

'A gentleman is not a tool'
(*Analects of Confucius*)

Since 1949 the quality of Chinese life has been shaped in the countries of the economic miracle principally by market forces and by the unplanned, at times random, action of all the individuals comprising a more or less 'free' society that embraces, save in Taiwan, alien races and 'pluralistic' cultures. In the People's Republic, the style of government has been opposite in nearly every respect; the quality of the body of men set apart to exercise 'the dictatorship of the proletariat' (by force and unrestrained by laws), the Party cadres, have been the key factor in the changing, or the stagnant, quality of the people's life. There are in any case eighteen million of them, outnumbering on one hand the population of Taiwan and on the other the Chinese inhabitants of Southeast Asia; in themselves, therefore, the cadres are one segment – one dare not say class – in the total quality of life; the major part of the stormy political drama since 1965 has been acted out on their smaller stage, with the masses onlookers or at most struggle-fodder. The early campaigns in the establishment of the Communist Party's total dictatorship over China were aimed at targets among the masses ('contradictions between classes'), but the targets of the Great Proletarian Cultural Revolution and its sequels under 'the Gang of Four' to reinforce Mao Tsê-tung's personal dictatorship ('contradictions within the people') have been located in the ranks of the establishment – in the same way as the victims of the 1930s purges by Mao's amanuensis, Stalin, after collectivization had cowed the Russian masses, were confined to the Soviet Party or the

71

Communist International. Although I had no contact with the
cadres thirty years ago, and did not find it opportune in 1979
to ask who was a Party member, and had therefore to rely on
guesswork from the deference shown to certain individuals,
the cadres merit a chapter as both agents and victims of the
contradictatorship (my word, not his) by which Mao brought
the country to its present condition.

For all the radical language of China's Marxist–Leninist
revolution, the cadres of today are in many respects spiritual
descendants of the 'mandarins' of imperial, the 'gentleman' of
Confucian, times. The political vocabulary of old China had
no single term for the institutionalized bureaucracy (the
world's earliest): like races who have hundreds of words for
fishes but none for 'fish', the Chinese had different terms for
their administrators viewed in different social relationships,
and over the centuries thousands of fanciful and undescrip-
tive titles for office and function, but no word for 'mandarin'.
Our European term arose as one of scores of Portuguese
oriental misapprehensions in the age of da Gama and
d'Albuquerque: the fidalgos heard Indian Brahmins talk
about *mantrin* 'a counsellor', confused it and the functions
implied with their own *mandar* 'to command', and gave the
world *mandarim* ('mandarin') for every kind of official in any
country east of Hormuz. Yet, applying this Sanskrit term to
the Chinese world was not infelicitous, for it is said that in
proto-historical times a *mantrin* had been a caster of spells, and
so too had the *ju* of proto-historical China who comprised the
'gentleman counsellors' of whom Confucius was the best
known and who became the 'mandarinate' of imperial times.
    For the mandarins to have commanded would have
amounted to overboiling the fish; they were invested with no
powers defined by law but were intended, by example and
exhortation, to dominate the masses and get them to live
according to conventions for a just and stable society handed
down, immutably, by previous generations. The recalcitrant could be punished – mostly with bastinadoing for want
of administrative means whereby to inflict other
punishments – according to a scale laid down for each offence
but without limitations on the mandarin's personal power to

sentence. If the Court got news of a crime wave in his jurisdiction, or if the crops failed, or still more assuredly if actual rebellion broke out, the mandarin could be made to answer personally (without right of self-defence) and be suspended, dismissed or even bastinadoed himself. The *esprit de corps* of the 'gentlemanly' élite one in 2500 of the population in Ou-yang Hsiu's day) was instilled in schools the 'elder born' ran themselves, and enforced since Han – that is, Roman – times through the hierarchy of examinations in literary rather than technical arts, which has proved one of China's gifts to the world as a whole but at which, in imperial times, perhaps one in 40 of the candidates passed at any attempt. Max Weber, author of *The Religion of China*, pointed out that China's examinations had something in common with ordination in a priesthood, conferring on the selected few who emerged as mandarins – sometimes after a lifetime of repetitive study of didactic literature in a terse and stilted language as remote from daily speech as Church Latin from Chaucer's English – an aura of magical 'virtue' in the eyes of the masses. Weber might have added that the ideogram for 'prose', at which it was essential to shine in order to graduate (*wên*), meant in the earliest age of writing the lines on the hand that are studied in palmistry, and that the 'virtue' of the proficient was handed down from those casters of spells of proto-historical times. Qualifying for the civil service was itself the play of chance, but one had to make believe it was a training and test carried out with discernment and fairness. Here is a defence of the arrangements (abridged), 'Why Study for the Civil Service?', composed at the time of Charlemagne by the T'ang dynasty mandarin and reformer of prose-style – typically, he called his innovation *ku wên* or 'ancient prose' – Han Yü, when challenged by a student protest:

It is morning, and the Elder Born enters the Great Hall. He makes a sign to his pupils to take their places below the rostrum and addresses them a homily on Mencius's text, '"Scholarship is refined by perseverance, but grows rank in idleness; character is formed by self-discipline – only infamy can come from self-indulgence." In the present age, it has befallen that the Sage Emperor and the Wise Minister have arisen together; government reaches out to the highest and the lowest, far and wide; the criminal and the wicked are rooted up and cast out, while the competent and the virtuous are promoted and honoured. . . . Though there may be men who get selected by good luck alone, who dare say there be one of many merits who is still unappreciated? So do you, my pupils, tax yourselves that your erudition does not achieve polish, do not blame those in authority for lack of perspicacity; tax yourselves that your conduct is imperfect, do not blame those in authority for unfairness.'

The end of the homily was never reached, for a scoff was heard in the ranks, and a sceptical voice protested: 'Does our Elder Born wish to humbug us? I have studied under him for several years now. His tongue is never still from harping on the refinements of the Six Arts, his hands tirelessly unroll and reroll the scrolls of the Hundred Schools in search of wisdom of deed or word. He has set himself a rigorous task and lets nothing tempt him away from its fulfilment . . . sparing neither tallow nor oil to prolong the hours of the sundial. If ever scholarship was persevering, it is our Elder Born's: he has gored every heresy with the sharp horns of his logic and tossed it into the dung. . . . And yet he receives no public recognition from the world at large, no private help from friends; every laborious step forward in his career has been followed by a backward stumble. . . . Imperial Censor for a while, he was soon banished among the southern barbarians [the Cantonese!] . . . Although he has passed out a Doctor of State three times, he has remained out of office and has had no chance to show his ability in government. His life has been plotted against by enemies, and repeatedly he has been brought to ruin. When the winter is mild, his children still cry with the cold; when the year is fat, his wife still complains of hunger. His pate has gone bald, and there are gaps in his front teeth; when he comes to the end of his days, what consolation will he have? And yet he goes on and on about following in his footsteps!'

'Come nearer, boys,' the Elder Born replied. 'From big tree trunks pillar and ridgepole are made, and from the branches the rafters are made; capitals and beams, architraves and dwarfs, doorsteps and threshold, lintels and frames have each the right timber, and sorting them out so that they make a building that will stand is the task of the master carpenter. Jade chips and powdered cinnabar, red-stalked mushroom and pale-green lichen, cow's urine and puff-ball, the rotted skins of spent drums – to collect and store all these medicines, prescribing them for the right disorders and never being out of stock, is the speciality of the learned physician. To ensure that the brilliant pass their examinations and that selections are made impartially, to select the clever from the stupid who are put up for advancement, and to inculcate precision in those who express themselves clumsily; to single out as models those who excel, to coax the shyness of some while checking the conceit of others, and to match rank with ability – all that befits the Chief Minister.... Though I may have been conscientious in my studies, I have failed to deduce the apodictic Truths; it is one thing to write good prose, another to have ideas to express in it. Nevertheless, every month I do spend my stipend of cash, every year I do consume my allowance of grain; my sons do not have to know how to till the soil, and my wife has never known what it is to have to spin.... If our discussion were to turn on whether I can show gain, and if our reckoning were to be based on whether my rank is honourable or less than I deserve – if I overlooked my own poor aptitude and pointed my finger at the blemishes of my seniors in office – that would be like reproving the master carpenter for not putting in a twig to hold the roof up, or giving the physician a bad name because he prescribes life-giving herbs instead of poisonous weeds.'

The tone of this genre of mandarins' prose is didactic to the point of priggishness; a lighter and more amiable side developed for a time, and an example will be found in 'Old Tipsy's Look-out' (see Appendix), but it died out three hundred years ago – possibly because of the rise of unofficial fiction – and Marxist–Leninist prose has reverted to homiletics even severer than Han Yü's. In this piece, the Elder Born's argument may well be specious, drawing the Court's attention to himself, but the text rated as a literary milestone in China down to my student days and is another example of continuity in political culture under Marxist–Leninist rule – not least striking details like the stock-in-trade of the 'physician' and the two-kind mode of remuneration. The underlying doctrine of unquestioning submission to what might be called apodictic justice – Lenin's aphorism 'Whatever the Party decides is a priori just' – is elaborated in the late Chairman Liu Shao-ch'i's exhortation to cadres:

> The leading body of the Party is empowered, on behalf of the membership, to give centralized leadership in the management of all Party affairs and to command obedience from the lower organizations and the Party membership. Order within the Party is built on the principle of the subordination of the individual to the organization, the subordination of the minority to the majority, the subordination of lower organizations to higher organizations, and the subordination of all the constituent Party organizations to the Central Committee.

The good Party cadre, he goes on, so disciplines himself that 'neither riches nor honours can corrupt him, neither poverty nor lowly condition make him swerve from principle, neither force nor threat of it bend him' – an unacknowledged quotation from Confucius known to every literate Chinese.[1]

The emphasis is on subordination and against personal initiative: the Court is always right, the Central Committee is always right. Two hazards above all others Han Yü and his students had to learn to submit to, making believe that all was well with the system of government: factional spite and rustication. Both those misfortunes have dogged the members of the Chinese Communist Party since 1949. Han Yü talks of 'matching rank with ability', but that did not mean that mandarins were intended to be specialists: instead, they were selected for supposed proof of moral capacity – of 'self-cultivation' in a phrase quite common in communist writing. The motto at the head of this chapter can be translated equally well 'the mandarin is not a specialist', and the idea behind it came to be that the successful graduate will be capable of correct judgement in any set of social, political or economic circumstances, by reason of the moral indoctrination he has given proof of in the examination; morality is a quality of the generalist, and 'virtue' (rewarded on retirement in the old days by presentation of a jade cup of pure water from a bubbling well) not the corruption of wealth must be sole guerdon of dutiful upholding of the 'system'. The Party's executives, its 'cadres', constitute a moral framework running through the whole structure of society and achieving socialist transformation through ethical precept; the Chinese translation for 'cadre', *kan pu*, has the same range of modern usages as the French and Russian original, but occurs already in Confucius's age to describe the identical function of 'gentlemen' in pre-imperial society.

Controversy over the degree of specialization the generalist mandarins ought to acquire arose repeatedly in the imperial period, and in mid-Sung became an issue of bitter strife. An influential body of opinion held that technical departments such as the Treasury or the salt administration ought to be headed by technicians promoted from the subordinate ranks of employees, 'lesser men', not by 'gentlemen' mandarins – very much the 1949 controversy in British colonies referred to in Chapter 1 over appointing doctors as directors of medical services or teachers as directors of education. Significantly for conditions in our time, Sung China gave the last word to the generalist mandarins. In spite of the efforts of Sun Yat-sen's Bolshevik advisers to make the Kuomintang a quasi-Communist Party of 'red' cadres, the pre-Liberation republic was evolving into a government of 'expert' civil servants under ministries working to regulation. Similarly, as one can see in every government office, Chinese public employees in communities outside China have taken without demur to service in administrations for which the training is professional and the duties specialized.

In Mao's China, controversy has raged again, over 'redness' against 'expertness', and degenerated into mortal struggle between revolutionary and technical factions. As in other communist parties in power, members join the Chinese Party because, having shown zeal at work or in subordinate masses organizations, they are invited to, not because they choose to, and promotion to be a cadre is on the same basis. Loss of favour and destitution from office has proved just as subjective: neither the old mandarinate nor the new Bolshevik-designed Party can be said to have laid down rules for discipline and punishment; that field has been, as it were, decentralized, like relations with the people, to absolute and arbitrary power vested in immediate superiors theoretically incapable of anything less than 'benevolence and justice', than 'class consciousness and political awareness'. There is no positive qualifying for advancement, only negative avoidance of disgrace. Without rules, the system lends itself to cliques – the bane of loosely-organized bureaucracies without definite and answerable chains of command the world over, and no less so of imperial, republic and now socialist China. Every generation has produced minds capable of diagnosing the ill, but the dogmatic intolerance which besets all Marxist–Leninist differences of opinion, coupled with the means of instant divulgation by radio, was bound to render today's struggles more immediate, more frequent, and more ferocious than China ever suffered in the past.

What was not so inevitable was Mao Tsê-tung's thirty-year-long harnessing of these spontaneous 'contradictions' as a tactical method by which gradually to tighten, first the Party's, later his own, dictatorship over the country; I mean the invention of government-by-mass-campaign, 'contra-dictatorship'. The cowardly persecutions and brutalities that have been perpetrated in China, from the land reform of 1951 through the anti-Rightist drive of 1958 to the Cultural Revolution of 1966 and after, have all been portrayed as the spontaneous action of the masses, not as the will of the Party 'centre'. In this particular make-believe lies perhaps the most cynical feature of the *divide-et-impera* on which Mao rested his rule. During the years of 'pacification' – another word that is as natively Chinese (*p'ing ting*) as it is French – the Party still had foreign well-wishers in its midst, who had accompanied the cadres and the Red Army (the same men) in the last phase of the civil war; those well-wishers have recorded, sympathetically, the process by which the Party brought villages under its domination, the rumble of its gunfire still reverberating in the peasants' memories. Having no idea who was who in the village, the cadres spent a few days in friendly and helpful conversation to spy out latent tensions and feuds; in order to 'exploit contradictions', they picked out 'temporary allies' –

usually starting with the poorest and working up the scale of 'middle peasants' till they built up a sufficient majority – and told them they constituted 'the revolutionary class' of the locality; a small number, preferably of those who owned something extra – it might be as little as one spare suit of clean clothes – were labelled (literally, with patches sown on the backs of their smocks) 'class enemies'. The stage was then set for public-denunciation 'struggles', alias 'people's courts', in which the majority had to shout abuse at the minority, whether over real extortion arising from the farming of the village's fields or over trumped-up paltrier tensions and jealousies. In districts occupied by the Red Army two or three years before proclamation of the People's Republic, the process was gone through a second time in 1951, the leaders of the first group of 'temporary allies' who had been left in charge now being relabelled by the cadres 'class enemies' in their turn 'pour mieux encourager les autres' – that is to say, in order to make doubly sure of loyalty to the new regime from a second group of more lasting allies.[2] Professor Lucian Pye has assembled evidence that such bullying of neighbours they had lived with all their lives, even if they did not get on with them, besides inculcating great circumspection, tended to outrage the sense of decency of the Chinese peasant 'strugglers'.[3]

In the country of the blind, the blindest man is king, and Mao Tsê-tung had even fewer ideas about the art of government in 1949 than his close collaborators had; the policies he inaugurated down to the time of his death were all attempts to govern by the tactics for revolution he had learnt during his formative years. It is recounted that, at the moment when Lenin sat down at his desk in the Kremlin on the first morning of Red October, he sighed that 'Marx gets us this far, but here he deserts us'. Mao might have sighed in his turn that Lenin had left him to his own devices. When the first Han Emperor had seized the imperial throne (in the age of Hannibal again), his chief minister felt obliged to warn him, 'Your Majesty has conquered the Empire on horse-back but you cannot rule from that posture.' Mao did not heed that hackneyed cautionary tale: he opted always for revolutionary 'red' methods that served personal dictatorship against administrative 'expert' ones that might have served the national economy, on the generalist against the specialist, on Lenin's 'voluntarism' (the will of the Party) posing as Marx's 'spontaneity' (the predicted joint action of a working class spurred by awareness of a common interest), and above all on Engels's insistence that 'terror' (Engels's word) is the essence of statecraft.

Contradictatorship fell with double harshness on the pre-Liberation intellectual establishment in the towns – professional men and women, teachers, and managers – because many of the ones who were not sent away to dig the reservoir at the San Mên Gorge or humiliated in other ways were actually appointed members of the Party to swell the ranks of the revolutionary cadres who had marched in from the civil war and only knew how to bivouac, or at least were allowed to carry on in their old positions with a revolutionary Party cadre beside them, in the way the Mongols supervised the Chinese mandarins in Kublai Khan's interest seven hundred years ago. Not only a large number of the new Party recruits – but also some of the older cadres who had worked for the Party in the 'white areas' behind the capitalist lines and had therefore escaped the cold showers of 'rectification of work-style' to which Mao periodically subjected the 'red areas' during the civil war – had to undergo courses of 'thought reform' to chasten their minds, stifle personal ideas about what ought to be done next, and ensure their automatic obedience to – if possible, anticipation of – the Leader's injunctions for management of state affairs.[4] Russian advisers were engaged for new industries, especially to help spend Russian money in accordance with the philosophy of economic development of the 1950s shared by the non-communist world in respect of Africa and other parts of Asia; Stalin's state system became the model for the New China in the same way as Britain's did for India.

But when the 'forces of production' in agriculture stayed 'unleashed' – perhaps became more 'leashed' still than under capitalism once individual rewards for labour had been abolished – Mao evidently suspected that the new cadres were to blame for adopting management methods appropriate to capitalism rather than to socialism: in spite of thought reform and the purges of the 'Three Antis' and 'Five Antis' in the towns at the time of the land reform in the country, there must lurk in Chinese society intellectuals still habouring counter-revolutionary thoughts. Thereupon he announced the 'Double Hundred' campaign – 'Let a hundred flowers bloom, let the Hundred Schools contend' (the hoary motto alluded to by Han Yü); free expression of ideas was permitted, criticism of the Party's policies encouraged. But only for four months; then the police swooped, and the more foolhardy and trusting spirits disappeared into the *gulag*, their periodicals tossed into the night-soil carts. I heard the first news of survivors being freed, together with the corpse of the author of *Rickshaw Boy*, during my stay in Peking twenty-two years later.

All one can say for the Great Leap Forward in 1958 is that it did not seem to purge anybody, but it had grave consequences for the quality of the people's material welfare. Disappointed with the performance of the steel industry, Mao ordered a mass campaign for building 'backyard furnaces'; the communes, just being organized, were, in an extravagance of decentralization in economic planning, henceforward to make their own steel. Spurred on by Party cadres ignorant of steel-making but well schooled in revolutionary zeal, the peasants stifled any private misgivings and beat the ploughshares nobody owned any longer into collectivized scrap iron on a vast scale, meanwhile neglecting the cultivation of the land nobody owned either so that the harvest declined still further but guzzling away at the free food in the commune kitchens. 'Self-reliance' was made the catch-phrase – not the self-reliance of all China *vis-à-vis* external trade and ideas, but self-reliance of each little production unit; over the next twenty years, this came to mean, in theory, dependence for capital on the collective's own savings without financial aid from the state, and in practice periodic destruction of one resource in order to 'fulfil a plan' to satisfy a current (to the ordinary man, arbitrary) Party line. On all hands, cadres and model workers, socially transformed, were supposed to be inventing 'advances in science and technology', and every month a film was made showing news of the most ingenious of them, for Party propaganda at home and to the Overseas Chinese. I used to watch these chronicles of the ridiculous in the government film-examiners' studio at Hong Kong – there was never anything to censor in the prim productions from the mainland – and remember an especially idiotic one about a contraption for hoisting building materials manually to the top of a chute and then letting them tumble down to their destination a few yards away; it was claimed that the 'breakthrough in dynamics' took less effort than pushing carts on the flat. The hearts of large numbers of educated Chinese must have sunk into despondency at the sight of these Social-Michurinist strides along the road towards . . . invention of perpetual motion?

Russian advisers too can be assumed to have been sarcastic; they were openly impatient with the Chinese Party's incompetence in carrying out Stalinist five-year plans – after all, their bureaucracy was able to boil the fish to a turn in their own empire, the extent of which was more than twice China's. Although the chief of Mao's many motives for finally breaking with the Soviet Union was almost certainly his annoyance at not being recognized in Moscow as *vozhd* over the international communist movement when Stalin died, a great many cadres will have been glad to see the Soviet advisers withdraw across the Gobi Desert, lock, stock and blueprints, in the footsteps of Borodin's Bolsheviks evicted by Chiang Kai-shek in 1927: first, native executives in any recipient government rarely welcome being observed, unless the advisers from the donor government establish complaisant relations by diverting some of the bounty to the executives' persons, whereas the latter in China dared not accept gratifications there was no way of spending or investing in the socialist market; and second, Chinese cadres would have stood to gain as well if Mao had become *vozhd* in the 1950s. Moreover, it is difficult to see how the Sino-Soviet dispute can in itself have harmed the quality of life of the Chinese masses. Be that as it may, Khrushchev's estimates of where Mao was leading China were borne out by events: by 1960, the discrepancy between the facts of famine and the statistical falsehoods published since 1957 were so glaring that the Chinese Communist Party decided to make the truth about production a state secret, not lifting the ban on publication until 1978. That secrecy could not have been maintained if Russian advisers had remained in the country. Mao was undoubtedly discredited to some extent: he relinquished the chairmanship of the state to Moscow-trained Liu Shao-ch'i – while retaining the more important chairmanship of the Party – and went into partial eclipse: the Sage Emperor handing over to the Wise Minister.

Mao spent much of his five-year 'retreat' not far from the Dragon's Well and, it would seem, devoted his mind, on one hand, to giving his quarrel with Khrushchev a philosophical cachet[5] and, on the other, to meditating on tactics for reasserting his despotism.

During Mao's temporary retirement, the quality of life in China underwent a measure of liberalization on the material side but, at least from the point of view of townspeople, also one of countervailing stringency on the political side. Under the latter, residents' committees were organized to control issue of ration coupons for food and clothing of persons not working on communes or in big factories, and at the same time to report to a Party cadre anything out of the ordinary in one another's behaviour; a similar system of mutual surveillance generally known as *pao chia* ('security shield') goes back to the time of Ou-yang Hsiu and was revived before Liberation by both Chiang Kai-shek and the Japanese military government in the coastal provinces. Here again was security firmly controlled in practice but ostensibly in the hands of the people themselves. In economic affairs, the Party delegated control to a growing hierarchy of state offices, substantially as well as nominally answerable to ministries rather than to local Party committees; the key figures in the hierarchy were themselves members of appropriate echelons of the Party, but, under the leadership of new State Chairman Liu, must have had fewer and fewer occasions for seeking or acquiescing in Politburo instructions.

Mao had to sit by idle while collectivization of agriculture – the very heart of his political thought in the eyes of many analysts, though not mine – was compromised by permission for the communes to assign up to a twentieth of their arable land to private plots, the products from which were saleable in open markets, while cereals – by production of which Marxists customarily measure the total economic success of their regime – began to be bought from capitalist Australia and North America. There is no telling whether the Chinese people's livelihood might have recovered at this stage from the effects of the Liberation itself, as well as from the Great Leap, if the new tendency to what Leninists call 'economism' had continued, or whether the capacity for production of consumer goods apart from food could ever have overhauled that of the other communist states – a result clearly essential before Mao could earn acknowledgement as *vozhd* over an international Marxist movement. It is certain, however, that socialist transformation looked like getting forgotten and Mao's supremacy at home threatened with further decline. In order to reimpose his will – his *volya* in the special usage of Lenin's 'voluntarism' – against the spreading tentacles of centralizing, bureaucratic government, he turned characteristically and logically to the familiar arts of revolution once more and, remounting his sinister hobby-horse, hit on the idea of the Great Proletarian Cultural Revolution.

The cadres, Party and non-Party, were the target of the fresh dose of revolution. A theoretical rationalization was afforded by ideas contained in Mao's essays of ten years before on 'contradictions', the gist of which (and to my mind the real heart of his Thought) was that local mutual hates dignified as class struggle are the sole dynamic of all societies, so that without them there can be no progress, and 'revolution' must continue permanently until Society reaches the last and perfect stage of development, namely true communism, and there is an end to progress. The final stage was still a long way off, not only in China, but also in the Soviet Union, and advance towards it must follow the stormy road of continuing class struggle – the opposite road to cooperation between classes, wickedly being urged as the 'correct' theory by Khrushchev, thwarter of Mao's world ambition. The proletariat must struggle perpetually against the bourgeoisie; but who was *that*? It was not dissidents or budding rivals for supreme power reported to Mao by an *Ogpu*, as the victims of Stalin's purges had been, for no such reliable administrative body existed in China; it was unknown persons whom the masses were to single out for themselves in application of a code for direction of 'the people's wrath'. The choice of individuals on which to pin the label of 'class enemy' had been made in the land reform by Party cadres, and the victims were members of the masses; this time roles were reversed, the victims being members of the establishment, whereas the 'strugglers' were from outside the hitherto sacrosanct Party – in the main, young and uninhibited schoolboys and girls, preferably from distant localities: in another Lenin metaphor, different times made different links in the chain of power the right ones to grasp single-mindedly for the moment. As with all Mao's contradictatorship campaigns, the object was not retribution for behaviour that was actually wicked: it was immaterial whether the culprits were guilty as charged, guilty of something else, or guilty of nothing at all; instead, the object was to chasten the thoughts of the 'strugglers' themselves, so that they would never dare entertain ambitions of their own for fear the same fate might await them. Under the new code, there were three qualifications for the label 'class enemy': first, one could be bourgeois by birth into a 'middle-peasant' or commercial family or because so labelled after the Double Hundred; second, one could be bourgeois by reason of current occupation – more or less anybody in the teaching profession and, above all, 'experts' who were managers and production-brigade leaders so determined to make a success of the undertaking entrusted to them that they could plausibly be accused of losing sight of the Enterprise of socialist transformation, accused of holding up material incentives to hard work instead of 'red' zeal, and therefore guilty of 'taking the capitalist road'; and third, the most luckless of all were individuals who happened to be present in an institution or enterprise when the 'strugglers' swooped on it or else were chosen because their neighbours or fellow workers were ordered to struggle *somebody* and there were absolutely no candidates in the first two categories on hand.

Mao started this Cultural Revolution to idealize Karl Marx's *lumpenproletariat* through the theatre, in which his very 'red' wife had been a professional failure and consequently was at loggerheads with art-for-art's-sake 'experts'. At first, the masses had cause to expect from this fact that 'culture' simply referred to questions intellectual – whether entertainment should be entertainment or propaganda. But the campaign in press and street posters (the original 'democracy walls') quickly switched to economic and political circles, culminating in the attack on Liu Shao-ch'i by office, though not by name – a coded message that nobody in the Party was above attack but that it was categories of people who should be gone for, without regard to personal guilt. In September 1980, the president of the reconstituted Supreme Court told the National People's Congress that, of the 270,000 individuals convicted by People's Courts as counter-revolutionaries at this time – apart, presumably, from the 40,000 murdered and the millions persecuted extra-judicially – 175,000 were not guilty of the facts alleged against them; another 26,000 convicted of factional association with Liu (goodness knows under what law!) were also innocent. Eventually, Liu was forced to name himself in a Stalinesque public confession and to accept responsibility for both extremism and excess of leniency in previous campaigns – for any 'line', in other words, that had proved unpopular. In universities, colleges and schools – chief purveyors of 'culture' – uncritical students and pupils were given the word to start 'criticizing' their teachers as bourgeois, and did so with such childlike vigour that many victims were physically maimed and a few bludgeoned to death; often bonfires were made of the contents of the libraries.

Next, all teaching institutions were closed, and the young men and girls mobilized as 'Red Guards' (a term revived from Lenin's assault force in the October Revolution). After a million-strong parade in Peking reviewed by the re-emerged Helmsman in his Manchester cloth cap, the Red Guards were sent forth, without paying on the trains, to 'storm the headquarters and seize power', in the name of Chairman Mao, in almost any part of the country – though not in the defensive belt along the Russian frontier or the central Asian minority areas where nuclear power was being developed. In a massive demonstration of their repudiation of all the things of the mind and all accepted standards of decency and consideration that were the only justification for their privileged education and were closely entwined in Confucianism, as Han Yü's essay illustrated, on the grounds that those things were not part of proletarian culture, the marauding hooligans smashed their way into government buildings (for example, the Foreign Ministry) and factories. The havoc there was even more far reaching than in the schools, although some workers improvised defences and fought the Red Guards off, inflicting casualties on them in revenge; in a few places army barracks were raided for weapons, and trains carrying Russian munitions for the communist side in the Vietnam war were looted. On the whole, communes were spared the jacquerie; the chief reason may have been merely that the rural areas were difficult to get to.

Soon the entire population was being required to demonstrate its proletarian culture: perhaps as the price for Mao's nomination of Lin Piao, veteran exponent of 'proletarian' people's war, to be his successor as Chairman, the People's Liberation Army tore off its badges of rank and showed that even the top general was but a simple soldier and worker at heart. The only books that were published from then on were the writings of Chairman Mao, and everybody had to carry round a copy of the 'little red book' of quotations which, with one eye on the Bible, purported to contain the whole of human wisdom in four hundred nutshells, so to speak, and with the other eye on Social Michurinism the key to Nature – that is to say, how by hating the right 'class enemies' as 'poisonous weeds' to make rubber-trees yield more latex or coalmines yield harder anthracite. On one hand people had to preface every observation they made in conversation at work with a trite commonplace from the red book, and on the other they had to 'struggle' one another with it in the paddy-field, on the shopfloor or across the yard of a block of flats. The cruel aspect of this wave of make-believe national lunacy was the order that wherever the masses were regularly mobilized for 'participation' in putting Party lines into effect – criticism and self-criticism meetings in communes and factories, neighbourhood meetings for preaching hygiene and birth control, and so on – the gathering had also to be used for 'struggling' some victim.

Once again, the influence of the Chinese language made itself felt. All personal given names in China are just ordinary words chosen for good luck, so that, besides the facility with which people can adopt second and even third names for themselves at different stages of their life, they are all the easier victims of nicknaming; one or two of our tourist guides actually preferred to tell us their nicknames (amiable ones) rather than their real names. That custom was now turned to account by the Red Guards to launch a spiteful demonology of vituperation without having to look the victims in the eye by naming their true names – a demonology owing more to inherited superstition than to acquired Marxism–Leninism. Thousands upon thousands of those picked on by the arbitrary procedures were not merely subjected to the indignity of wearing dunces' caps for the duration of the meeting but were thereafter, at best, drafted indefinitely to retrieval of the night-soil in the workplace they formerly had charge of, at worst sent to unknown destinations to do forced labour; Party cadres suffered most. The rump of the territorial administration and judicial fraternity, sadly depleted in previous campaigns, now sank for the third time – into the *gulag*. Buddhist and Christian churches and the mosques of Central Asia had been forced years before to come to terms with the Party on the basis of Marxism–Leninism first, religious faith second – which is customary in communist states; now their holy places were broken into, religious objects desecrated, stolen or smashed, and the clergy sent away as class enemies; only one church was kept open in Peking for attendance by foreigners, and four or five pagodas were preserved in other cities for the edification of visiting foreign dignitaries, but without performance of rites, the greater number of the edifices – not a few of which were national monuments – being abandoned to weather and time. Most astonishing of the acts of vandalism was the demolition, complained of by the Peking press, of twenty miles of the Great Wall.

Places of alien worship, even the Great Wall, did not matter, but barracks and factories did: order had to be restored if the nation was not going to be struggled back into the stone age. The masses were not told whether the reversal of line originated with the Helmsman or with his new deputy, Lin Piao, but after eighteen months and a thorough dislocation of the Party hierarchy, the army was moved in to stem by force the national decline into chaos. The Red Guards were the first of Mao's latest 'temporary allies' to be rounded up, the younger ones sent home but the elder ones drafted to state farms to labour. For several years before, graduates from institutions of tertiary education had been sent off for periods of rustication – the slogan 'up to the mountains and down to the villages' – portrayed as the socialist honour of putting their technical training at the disposal of ignorant peasants, but at the same time benefiting as New Men from the peasants' more practical view of nature and style of life. The policy was an aspect of Social Michurinism, designed to level out the differences between worker and peasant in both standard of living and value system – precisely one of the visible achievements of the economic miracle, unplanned, in Hong Kong and Taiwan – and the idea was that the young cadres would marry locally and 'proletarianize' the rural areas in a sense close to Cicero's when he coined the word.[6] Occasionally, such marriages did take place, but mostly the peasants resented the rusticates as parasites, while the rusticates failed to adapt to rough living and demanded (and usually got) subsidies from the town Party committees which had rusticated them. That seems to have been the fate in due course of the majority of Red Guards. Rustication has continued as a policy, and during my few days in Shanghai in 1979 I witnessed two demonstrations by rusticates (pathetic in numbers and arousing no reaction from bystanders), apparently in support of a poster on one of the democracy walls demanding an end especially to the compulsory marriages that were an element in rustication.

After the removal of the Red Guards, the schools and universities were not reopened for periods ranging from two to ten years: they stayed shut in part as a security precaution, in part for lack of teachers able and willing to return to their posts. The formula for restoring order after the Cultural Revolution was the vesting of authority in every commune, factory, institute, district and province in a 'revolutionary committee' comprising (in a Khrushchevian *troika*) soldiers, 'experts' from the struggled establishment (who alone knew where the keys were kept, for example), and 'reds' from the struggler faction of the locality; the soldiers were always in the chair. In many places it took another year or two before sufficient harmony could be counted on between the literally mortal enemies of the previous months to sit down together in collaboration; but, whatever confusion reigned at lower levels, Mao Tsê-tung was firmly back at the helm. The army too now found itself a mere temporary ally, and by 1971 it was victim in its turn of a 'seizure of power': Lin Piao allegedly plotted his own *coup d'état* to hasten Mao off the throne, was found out, fled towards the Soviet Union in a Vickers Viscount, but crashed in the Mongolian Republic. The manner of Lin's death is certain, but the rest of the story may be fabricated; in any case, it was the signal for a further wave of power struggles within revolutionary committees that must have left the masses deeply bewildered.

Mao was ageing fast but was managed by his wife and the other three members of the Gang of Four; the upshot of their intrigues was supersession of the soldiers by a new generation of 'red' cadres and, incidentally, the secret killing of Liu Shao-ch'i – not by culpable bullet but by unattributable exposure without clothes to winter weather. In complete repudiation of Liu's economism, the 'reds' vowed they were dedicated to extreme egalitarianism in remuneration for labour and in distribution of consumer goods and social resources; but, since Mao's death, it has come to light that they were in reality as devoted as backsliding mandarins of old to pursuit of status and wealth, though not of course invested wealth. Their protestations of radicalism in some provinces (for example, that of Hangchow) were a make-believe for dismemberment of agricultural communes and reversion to private cultivation of all the land, not just the private plots. The most grievous backsliding was in regard to what might be called *prerogative*: cadres of the 'red' faction, as well as army officers who had hypocritically discarded their pips, abused the masses' fear of them to appropriate to themselves the houses and movable property that constituted 'fruits of struggle' and that in the land reform would have been divided among the local underprivileged; in Peking, former ministry buildings were requisitioned in the name of 'revolutionary committees' as if by any army of occupation. A sexual dimension of 'embourgeoisement' through exercise of prerogative came to light just after my visit, when a girl on a commune committed suicide, apparently under menace of *droit de seigneur*: the middle-aged leading Party cadre of the day had used his control over her livelihood and bondage to her place of work to force her to marry (on the face of it) his son; under the decentralized, collectivized regime, the girl had no laws or government agencies to turn to for help – she could only make a public scandal. The culprit of this particular abuse was punished in the same arbitrary fashion, without a hearing, in a manner and to a degree that suited the Party's public relations of the moment. Several women refugees have told of *droit-de-*

seigneur experiences like that in recent years, and the buying and selling of little girls continued long after Liberation;[7] socialist transformation has not changed *their* quality of life radically since the days of my Ipoh *mui tsai*.

6   The Chinese Intellectual Crisis

> 'Our most unfounded self-deception of the present day is to denigrate Western civilization as "materialistic" and to glorify Oriental civilization as "spiritual" '
>
> (Hu Shih, philosopher and originator of the 1917 Literary Renaissance)

My wife and I had not penetrated more than fifty yards into People's China before we came upon slogans proclaiming the urgency of 'modernization' as post-Mao China's order of the day – the Four Modernizations: that is of agriculture, of industry, of technology and of defence. The slogans implied a reversal of the immediately-preceding intellectual attitude enjoined on the masses, and yet they were not so different from the order of the day in far-off 1949: as soon as Mao was defeated in the civil war, Chiang Kai-shek promised to embark on just such a policy, and some Chinese today point to the economic miracle of Taiwan as an earnest in retrospect of his sincerity. But there is a lot more to the question than that: the Chinese people have been arguing about modernization for a hundred and fifty years, and their success in equipping themselves for the task intellectually during the half century from about 1890 to 1940 was remarkable – exceeded perhaps only by that of the Japanese, who led the way for all peoples, including the Koreans and Vietnamese, who share the common Confucian culture, vocabulary, and way of writing.

Modernization has involved a conceptual and linguistic revolution, and the rapid coinage of expressions for Western philosophy and science in the last century, entirely from Chinese roots yet of perfect accuracy, has been a cultural feat commanding respect and admiration; the fact that none of the

Sinic languages differentiates plural from singular, past from future, conditional from actual has proved no impediment to adoption of scientific method. During those decades, not only did the general body of Western knowledge percolate to lower and lower levels of Chinese society in the home country and through those Overseas communities that kept up communication with home, but Chinese intellectuals became witnesses of, and soon participants in, scientific, social and political developments in the West as those took place; for a large body of Chinese, Western ideas ceased to be felt to be alien. One important example was the development of medical knowledge and practice, another the invention of the mass-circulation newspaper: the latter made its appearance in Chinese urban life as soon as it did in Western, the former with varying delays of the order of ten or a dozen years. None the less, whether the Chinese perception of Western ideas was one of observation or one of participation, it led the Chinese nation into an intellectual crisis of cultural identity not resolved by 1940 and evidently felt just as acutely today by the Party leaders who have enunciated the latest 'line'. For all that the Overseas Chinese more than Europeans have been the bringers of modernization to the native peoples of Southeast Asia, my impressions of their society today made me wonder whether the crisis has been resolved there either.

The problem might be summed up as a quest for modernity without mundanity. The first awareness of a need for more advanced technology came to China's ruling class from the shock of what are conveniently, if inaccurately, called the opium wars. Superior naval vessels and firepower rendered European gunboat diplomacy invincible, and that alone was at first the limit of Chinese self-doubt. The remedy required 'specialists' trained in mathematics, physics, engineering and so on, but only after their minds had been formed in the pedantic classical learning. With European technical assistance, mostly paid for at a high price, the Chinese government of the day accomplished major changes in its modernization of armed forces, especially the navy, and in building up a munitions industry. There was unfortunately no commensurate improvement in political capacity in defence of the realm, not least because the Court was regarded, and regarded itself, as foreign: defence of Manchu rule became a more compelling imperative as the established order came increasingly under attack from rebels able to buy firearms for themselves from the foreigners crowding into the treaty ports whose 'open door' was the chief capitulation imposed by gunboat diplomacy.

It dawned on China's 'gentlemen and mandarins' only gradually that their ancient civilization might have something to learn from Western barbarians in things of the mind as well as the technology of war. The comforting thought that Western technology, especially armaments, could be dismissed as 'materialistic' and therefore no match in the scales of time for the 'spiritual' values of Chinese culture died hard; it received a fresh tonic from a visit the Bengali poet Rabindranath Tagore paid to China in 1921, calling forth Hu Shih's rebuke at the head of this chapter. Hu Shih went on to point out that the humanitarianism of the West must be accounted 'spiritual', bound feet and *mui tsais* 'materialistic'. To some extent, the intellectuals' perception of the two cultures was clouded by religion: Europeans, however shaky the historical grounds, pointed to the Christian faith as the source of and justification for the whole of their philosophy, including social philosophy and politics, and even, in the case of the Jesuits, for their scientific knowledge. Arguments from faith in preference to utility were unlikely to appeal at all to protagonists of such a self-conscious system of society and government as the Confucian; but, in any case, if a religious justification was the right one to postulate, then the Buddhist faith stood on an equal footing with the Christian and was better assimilated.

In the end, however, many concluded that modernization of Chinese life for the sake of the survival of the national state called for modification, and even abandonment, of elements in Chinese culture. But which ones? Could China have major engineering works without engineers who had devoted *all* their study years to mathematics and physics, or have competent engineers without a wide school catchment, a wide-enough school catchment without a change in attitudes over schooling for the lower classes? Could one have motor transport without a rule of the road, a rule of the road without police and magistrates, a civil code and compensation? Could one count on men of initiative and sense of responsibility to carry out modernization for defence or wider purposes within the inflexible Confucian ideology that depreciated originality and brooked no questioning? Or might freedom of thought prove indivisible? The Literary Renaissance and the clear-language movement which Hu Shih carried through in collaboration with the Trotskyist Ch'ên Tu-hsiu still did not resolve the basic dilemma. Indeed, could it have been resolved by education alone, or did the centuries-old political institutions have to be scrapped as well?

The last question was answered by the gun. Still, as we saw in the last chapter, tradition and political culture live on both among the Chinese masses and among the leaders of the would-be radical upheaval, and consequently the first question remains unanswered. Only the Marxist–Leninists have declared themselves willing to reject the whole national past – to accept the dissolving of any Chinese characteristics found to stand in the way of modernity into an undiscriminating mundanity, not of free thought, but of an international culture without frontiers but rigidly circumscribed intellectually: 'Nationalism is degenerate,' *The Polemic* quotes approvingly from Stalin's *Questions and Answers*, and the Chinese revolution is but a stage in world revolution. The Thought of Mao Tsê-tung[1] has sometimes been interpreted in the West as aimed at 'sinification' of Marxism–Leninism – at giving it an essentially Chinese flavour; but that interpretation mistakes the tactics of revolution, as Mao planned them in the 1930s, for the strategy of government he intended to follow in power and ignores the bowdlerization since 1949 of the word 'sinification' from newer editions. Mao did not prescribe government by permanent revolution and mass campaign, in opposition to the bureaucratic Stalinist state, for the Chinese masses alone, but for the workers of the whole world; national liberation under Chinese guidance was *The Polemic*'s programme for effecting it. Couching Mao Thought in formulas of the kind of 'The Ten Relationships', modelled on the Confucian 'Seven Relationships', was a tactical mode of communication, as was Liu Shao-ch'i's incorporation, during the 'sinification' years (1939), of sentences from Confucius side by side with sentences from Lenin or Stalin. That traditional literary conceit came to an end anyway with the 'Down with Confucius' campaign in 1974.

The Manchu Court dragged its feet over the modernization

of education – over such measures as cutting back on classical studies in favour of mathematics and science which at the time were being opposed, be it remembered, in Britain as well as China – because the ideological foundations of the monarchy would be undermined. After the republican revolution in 1911, political imperatives continued to constrain harmoniza- tion of traditional values with the social requirements for modern technology, but they were external imperatives now, coming from Russia and Japan, which did not so much obstruct the process in China as try to get its direction into their hands. The Chinese in Taiwan claim today that they have resolved the old dilemma at last, in spite of unremitting external constraints on them arising from the threat of invasion from the mainland and the necessity of conforming their policy to the value system of the Western allies on whom they still rely for support against such an invasion. Remember- ing on my 1979 tour that in 1949 I had found Taiwan still heavily marked by its half century of Japanese rule, I looked for outward signs to support the claim; what I saw is described topically below.

The intellectual crisis was felt quite acutely by the Overseas Chinese in the 1940s; in the minds of my applicants for naturalization as British subjects, their unease arose in part from it. For the Chinese in Southeast Asia there are three elements that have to be harmonized: the modernization of knowledge, the Chineseness to which they naturally cling in alien surroundings, and the concessions they must make to the culture – at the very least, the language – of the other races they live among and who demand the bigger voice in shaping the joint political and social institutions of the new states. 'Chineseness' for them largely means models taken from Chiang Kai-shek's China of the 1930s through the popular schools opened in every little town at that time on the initiative of trade guilds and chambers of commerce. At the beginning of the 'people's war' in Malaya, I was made a watchdog over subservsion in Chinese-language schools: the teachers were vociferous about the threat from Malay domi- nance that decolonization posed for their language and culture, as it did for the merchants' commerce; the com- munists took up the cry and egged on the pupils, especially in Singapore, to riot on the pretext of it. In 1952, one of the teachers' associations invited me to give a public lecture in Chinese airing my views on their dilemma. I argued that the remarkable conceptual adaptation of their language was a never-ending process, that the home country could hardly be looked to for inspiration in future because Mao had put 'socialism before patriotism' and was already burning the books of the old learning (with worse to come), and that, unless they could train youngsters to man the professions or become journalists and technicians able to provide literature and knowledge cast to the Southeast Asian environment for a new class of artisan or manager, they must expect young Chinese with English education to overtake them, with ultimate loss altogether of the Chinese traditions they cherished. That the problem was indeed widely felt was confirmed when all three Chinese dailies took my text and printed it on the same day and, a little later, when the communists' jungle broadsheet, *Freedom News*, lambasted me as a running dog of the imperialists. Here too then it should be possible to find signs in 1979 to show whether the enduring intellectual crisis had been resolved.

It would be impossible to devise a comprehensive scale for measuring the state of development in mainland China today applicable to all of the Four Modernizations. Superficially, there are abundant signs of what Marxist–Leninists and some others call 'unequal development': on one hand there are those 'human camels' lugging loads on carts through the streets and an agriculture still fertilized to upwards of ninety per cent by old-fashioned nightsoil, and on the other locally-copied Rolls-Royce jet engines, advanced nuclear plants, and indigenous design and manufacture of ballistic missiles – on one hand acupuncture and barefoot herbalists, on the other world leadership in microsurgery. The Overseas Chinese do not have to put up with the backwardnesses in my examples, but their societies are not capable of the advances either, even if their leaders can plead that that may be because the biggest of them is barely a hundredth of the size of China proper. The feature that is most striking about the contrast in the People's Republic is that, as with the rights and duties discussed in Chapter 4, the advances are at best of collective benefit, the backwardnesses borne by individuals – not excluding the field of medicine, where beneficiaries of advanced skills are chosen according to cadre-status or else with an eye to the Party's prestige and not according to Western notions of 'medical need'.

It is harder still to reach a judgement about the extent of the general knowledge of the people in different Chinese communities. Outside China, there are few impediments to acquisition of general knowledge, news of events in the world at large, exposure to social, political and philosophical ideas; mainland publications are still banned in Taiwan and were subject to examination at one time in most Southeast Asian countries, and now and then an issue of a foreign periodical containing hostile material about the local government is liable to be censored, but the coming of the transistor wireless and the television have rendered these residual restrictions from the cold war of less and less effect. One gets a different feel in the People's Republic: there, the level of general knowledge is low, and the initiative to publish it through reference books, periodicals, newspapers and radio which is open in the outside world is still wholly blocked by the political system; news of external events has been kept down to the level of thirty years ago, before modern media of communication were available in China; and Marxism–Leninism–Mao Tsê-tung Thought has been the sum total of ideas of which even intellectuals have heard for many years. An example of the Party's news management arose when I was in Peking: our guides heard about the Liberation Army's invasion of Vietnam from us, and when, belatedly, the Party newspapers did divulge that it had taken place, the presentation was wholly polemical, justifying the action, with a minimum of information about the battles, and certainly none at all prompted by news-for-news's-sake. I was able a few days later to observe the presentation of the same news in first a school and next a factory: in both places communication was by chalk drawing executed by the staff propagandist on a blackboard fixed to the wall for the purpose. The caricature drawings were both well done, but the message was merely a long denunciation of the Vietnamese Communists as puppets of the Soviet Union. Obviously what I was looking at was the normal procedure for spreading loaded news from the only source allowed to exist in the country – one which the Party admitted, shortly after I got home, 'is too often both dull and untruthful'.

I was told that in the south, since the fall of the Gang of Four, a minority of individuals who can afford private transistor sets or televisions and rejoice in privacy in their homes tune in to Hong Kong or Taiwan, but the effect of the change cannot have reached far yet. I found the leading Peking and Shanghai bookshops to be but shadows of their 1948 counterparts: in both the biggest section was for children's books, the next biggest manned by four or five idle assistants offering editions of Mao and the Four Sages, another for sale of political posters, and the fourth for technical books strictly practical in content (elementary civil engineering, machine-minding and mending, draughtsman's tables, do-it-yourself medicine), with no theoretical science books to be seen; there were no classics – only one or two pre-Liberation authors who died soon enough to be hailed as precursors of Mao, unlike the unlucky ones who stayed alive and, to a man or woman, ended in the *gulag* if not the grave. Certainly, one of our older guides – one I felt sure had only recently been rehabilitated himself – showed awareness that general knowledge in China is relatively limited, but young people probably do not feel any deprivation.

Press debates prove that, outside the two or three professions protected from struggle during the Cultural Revolution, the Chinese educated classes to whom it falls now to plan the Four Modernizations are conscious of the leeway they have to make up in the quality of their *work* as much as their own and the masses' life. When I asked at least to look inside the great library at Hangchow which catches the eye from every angle of the West Lake, picturesque heart of that ancient capital, I was told it was shut for good; presumably, when the Red Guards demanded admission, the learned contents had been more kindled than kindling. Only last year, the newly-revived Academy of Social Sciences was appealing to fellow professionals in Western countries to let them have duplicates of international periodicals to replace the copies systematically destroyed in the name of the working class: like the caliph in the apocryphal story of the burning of the Library of Alexandria, the Red Guards judged that any idea in these serials that was not in the little red book was heretical, and if there was none the serials were superfluous, so that in either case they ought to be burnt. On the technical side, it can be assumed that the availability of talent for repair and future development will vary enormously and fortuitously from region to region and from vocation to vocation – for instance, a gap reported in 1979 between backward methods in mining iron ore and advanced methods in newly-installed blast furnaces – but there are also intangible barriers to quick recovery facing implementation of the Four Modernizations.

In the first place, those fields where recovery depends on learning from abroad must be held back by the even more severe depletion of ranks under the influence of xenophobia: merely to be in the habit of reading technical books in English was to incur risk of spiteful condemnation as a foreign spy in the judgement of strugglers spurred by proletarian ignorance. In the second place, the confidence that can be placed in the present leaders and their liberalizing policy must be tempered by experience: there is no certainty that after they leave the political scene – and Têng Hsiao-p'ing, the current power-behind-the-Chair, for all his sprightly gait and Stetson hat on television, is an old man – there will not be a reversion to the Mao-Thought threat of continual (if not exactly continuous) revolution in the special sense of contra-dictatorship. In the third place, as recently as the spring of 1980 it was demonstrated that the priority of security of the regime over modernization is as positive as it was in the opium wars: a research department in the coal industry was shut down and the scientists put on shovelling the coal – 'not an isolated case', *People's Daily* added. It is not surprising that rehabilitated experts coming abroad talk warily. Contrariwise, the 'red' management cadres who for so long have been associated with the purges are themselves threatened now: Têng Hsiao-p'ing and Hua Kuo-fêng have both retired ostentatiously from high offices of state, setting an example 'right down to basic units' for ending the notion of an establishment of Party cadres: Party seniority, Hua declares (quoting, astonishingly, Andrew Jackson!), will no longer earn promotion, survival of the Long March no longer qualify for direction of a university, for chairmanship of a municipality or an industrial ministry, even for management of a commune. But can this commonsense measure be trusted to last? Or is it another arbitrary decision of the kind that all along has made the cadre's quality of life as worrying as that of Han Yü and all the mandarins in between? The following tale, broadcast in 1978, testifies to arbitrariness still in the name of the very 'regularization' (that is, introduction of rules) Hua instituted the previous year, *inter alia*, to curb banquets and gallivanting at communal expense:

> Chêngkuan Township Party Committee organized a group of thirty-seven cadres to visit Tachai [a commune long cited (not least by Hua) as a model of self-reliance but today shown up as a fraud; at the time the story unfolds, lip service still had to be paid to the make-believe]. They went by train to Yangchuan in Shansi and from there by bus to Hsi-yang. On arrival at Tachai, they spent only one day rushing round a few of the brigades, and then boarded the train for Peking, where they gave half a day to studying market-gardens in the suburbs but two and a half days to the tourist sights. Next they went to Chufu in Shantung for a hasty briefing on intercropping, before a leisurely tour of the tomb and temple of Confucius. Next they reboarded the train, ostensibly to study pig-raising in Chêkiang; but, after stopovers at scenic spots like Wusih and Soochow, they were too tired and instead cruised by river steamer back up the Yangtze, with one stop for sight-seeing at Wuhan, and so home to Chêngkuan. The 2500-mile journey cost the public purse £1500. Eventually the facts leaked out, and the culprits were ordered to confess, under mass-criticism, at a succession of struggle meetings. . . . It is known that this sort of thing is going on all over the country, and so the humiliation of the culprits by which the Party has upheld state law in this case is being published as an example to all.

The literary cast of the story might have been Ou-yang Hsiu's, but alas for socialist transformation: the hammer blows of Mao's extremist Social Michurinism seem hardly to have dented human nature.

No chapter and verse was given for the law laying down

'struggle' as a punishment, but by the time I got to Peking there was plenty of talk of more exact rules to give effect to 'Great Order across the Land'. In January 1980 new codes were enacted (not debated) by the National People's Congress covering the whole range of penal and civil law and the attendant procedure, in replacement at last of the pre-Liberation ones repealed thirty years ago – from which they do not differ profoundly, so that, in theory at least, what the Chinese citizen can do, and what can be done to him, is now similar whether he lives in the People's Republic or on Taiwan. It would be expecting too much, however, to assume that the Party's old security apparatus, owing nearly as much to tradition as to Marxism–Leninism, is going to disappear from every town, village and commune overnight and be replaced by a newly-trained police force and new courts suddenly dedicated to 'modern' ideals more alien than those of Marxism–Leninism and daring not to look over their shoulders all the time for signs of the wishes of the local Party committee. Citizens' rights under the 1978 Constitution no longer include 'equality before the law' and 'freedom of residence' which had been written into the 1954 Constitution and deleted in 1975; the late deletion, long after their abolition in practice, does not bode well for criminal-procedure rights that are now being restored under the appropriate code. Class struggle is still a foundation-stone of the state, and the Constitution still sanctions 'ideological remoulding through labour', so that there is conflict between codes and Constitution.

But it may only be a few intellectuals who worry about that. On none of the democracy walls in the towns I visited did I see texts that called the system of government, or its ideology, in question; the faces scanning them eagerly but enig-matically – in reply to my questions I could only get nods and smiles, but was that due to my clumsy mandarin speech? – may have reflected no more than sympathy with the grievances bemoaned, not doubt about, still less hostility to, Marxism–Leninism. I can draw no conclusion, except to infer that, since the democracy walls have since been wiped clean by the authorities, the whole unofficial literature that had flourished since Mao's death been suppressed, and Wei Ching-shêng, chief protagonist of both, been sentenced to fifteen years for counter-revolution (even though he did not question Party rule either), toleration is still not meant to extend beyond criticism of the implementation of Party lines. Chinese people are bound to feel it is still rash to show initiative or ambition or actually to exercise any freedom the Communist Party accords them in principle.

Our guides in China made no bones about the 'proletarian' closure of schools, colleges and universities – some of the latter not open again at that time: a generation of technicians had been lost, because even at the lower-level institutions which, less likely to harbour independent thought, had reopened earlier, admission had been on grounds of 'redness' in the struggle movements and not by examination of previous attainment. Examinations were just beginning to take the place of sponsorship by influential cadres – a reform necessitated by the same abuse, on the part of mandarins, countless times under the emperors. At the one school I was shown round, the lack of educational progress in teaching methods during the previous thirty years was patent: even the three 'junior middle' classes (now reckoned an extension of primary school in both the People's Republic and Taiwan, as it happens) were still being taught entirely by rote, tried and true stifler of initiative, from what the unmodernized teacher wrote on the blackboard.

I expected to hear, but did not – perhaps because at bottom this, like everything else, is a political question in the eyes of the Party – hints of regret over the mutilation under Mao Tsê-tung's auspices of the Chinese written characters. The pretext is proletarian, no-nonsense simplification and lightening of the burden mere literacy imposes on children; yet the practical gain, judged numerically, is but an eighth, from reduction of 214 symbols corresponding to our letters to 187, whereas on the debit side children will be blinded ('not to know the characters is to be blind', said the old Thousand-Character Classic) to traditional books banned from their classrooms in 1966 – no doubt the real purpose. Even carefully-written wall posters conformed to the new style and were, like the latest printed books, set out in horizontal lines from left to right instead of the old vertical columns read from right to left. I found the mutilated characters officially adopted in Singapore and Macau and in use in Malaysia; both systems are used in Hong Kong, but Taiwan naturally forbids the communist forms. I only saw the old characters in Thailand, but had nothing to go by in Indonesia. Unhappily, mutilated characters are not the end of the proletarian revolution in writing in Maoist minds: next will come romanization of the Chinese language – not in the well-established Wade–Giles ('unequal-treaty'?) system, but in a would-be phonetic system, hideous to the eye and unpronounceable to the mind's mouth; it is a jumble of *x's* and *q's* having inconsistent and recondite values and plainly chosen out of contempt for the values bourgeois foreigners put on the letters. At first I thought the public notices bearing the new spellings were meant for foreigners who did not know characters, but I was told that one day they will become the standard writing. The needs of mechanization and computerization might seem to justify the intellectual vandalism; yet there were movable types in China four hundred years before Gutenberg, and there is already in existence a basic computer vocabulary of three thousand characters that is sure to be added to. (The total number of characters given in the standard K'ang Hsi dictionary of 1721 is about 44,000.)

My Southeast Asian teachers' anxiety in 1952 about the future of the Chineseness of their schools is coming to pass. In Singapore, English has largely displaced Chinese, not because of official policy but from a radical change in parent choice – the belief that English opens more doors to knowledge and careers than Chinese, whereas ties with the homeland are of greatly diminished importance to their lives, especially under the fettered intellectual regime there. The Nanyang (Southeast Asia) University, opened under Lin Yü-t'ang, author of *My Country and My People*, at the time of my public lecture in order to carry out a programme of modernized studies in Chinese very like what I was advocating, has had to capitulate to fashion and merge with Singapore's English-speaking university, accepting that English has become the sole vehicle for tertiary education for all Overseas Chinese. In Malaysia too, Chinese education is moribund, but by government fiat: in countries where the Chinese are a minority, host governments have tried to assimilate them through their children's schooling – more accurately *dissimilate* them from solidarity with China, since the Malays, for instance, would not welcome uncircumcised citizens into the bosoms of their families. The basic instrument for assimilation is the language of instruction, and so in Malaysia all schooling has to be in Malay, with English and Chinese taught as foreign tongues to Chinese children who speak them at home. Chinese engineers and doctors who have only read Malay books are hard to imagine, but such is the plan. In Thailand and Indonesia, Chinese lessons are ruled right out by the authorities, and English predominates in secondary and tertiary education. By contrast, the British authorities in Hong Kong are phasing out government finance for English schools in favour of Chinese ones, but for those who can pay – and even in People's China there are school fees to pay – there is a choice of schools of various persuasions, including communist ones, and various qualities, as well as both English and Chinese universities. My impression of Taiwan education is of high quality in technical subjects – although textbooks in shops were translations or adaptations, rarely original – but of less satisfactory standards in literary and social-science subjects though free from the ideological tyranny of the mainland.

My prediction to the teachers that, after the preliminary 'burning of the books' in the People's Republic (perpetrated the first time by Mao's historical hero, the Great Unifier, in 215 BC), worse must be to come was based on the belief that aesthetics and absolutism must prove incompatible: appreciation of art is personal and therefore a rival, wherever it occurs, to the high revolutionary purpose that is the same as the despot's sway. That Mao Tsê-tung may not have been a philistine in his youth, as was his model Stalin, rests in the main on early poems like the one usually called 'Snow'; celebrating his first glimpse in 1936, after the Long March, of the wastes of North China, 'Snow' is in blank verse but expressed in classical vocabulary as abstruse as Han Yü's, if of vivid imagery and sensitivity; yet six years later, after he had time to read Lenin and Stalin thoroughly, Mao was describing to the Forum on Art and Literature at Yenan (his revolutionary 'capital') the function of artist and writer, in his social and political system, on lines which did not play down or even reject aesthetics but ignored it altogether. The regime's gradual tightening of control over artistic expression matched exactly the tightening of Mao's dictatorship and ended in the purge of every one of the pre-Liberation left-wingers who had worked for the Party's victory, or at least against its defeat.

Simon Leys has pointed out Peking's use of archaeological exhibitions abroad to cover up neglect and destruction of national monuments, and I read for myself the explanations for Chinese visitors on the exhibits at the Historical Museum and the Ming Tombs: all of them ignored the aesthetics of the objects and concentrated on lessons about the labour of the masses dissipated in their production; the subliminal inference must be that beauty is inseparable from slavery. Besides 'Snow', Mao wrote a lot of platitudinous doggerel while he totally suppressed spontaneous poetry by other people, and the airport lounges are plastered with giant reproductions of his own ugly scrawl demonstrating his contempt for China's premier art of painting and calligraphy. A kind of rehabilitation from proletarian depredations is afoot today in this field as in others – monuments like the tomb of Genghis Khan are being restored, 'learned' societies are being started in provincial towns; but everything is under strict Party direction, the Double Hundred is to be allowed only in subordination to politics, and competitive 'expertness' in art is encouraged only in the common service of the Four Modernizations. 'At present certain comrades set emancipating the mind against upholding the Four Modernizations, regard breaking into forbidden areas as the same as bourgeois liberalization, and interpret paying attention to social effects as "retraction" in principles and policies. These are one-sided subjectivist, that is, individual ideas ... out of tune with Marxism – Leninism – Mao Tsê-tung Thought.' The miserable fact is that the last thirty years have seen grow up a whole generation of literate, if not educated, Chinese for whom aesthetics is an unknown expression of the human spirit.

Chinese art and literature do not thrive conspicuously outside the People's Republic either, but the reasons are to be sought in the smallness of the Southeast Asian communities and the rootlessness of Hong Kong – certainly not in political repression. Even in Taiwan, I discovered, although I could not find those pre-Liberation left-wing authors on sale in the bookshops of Taipei either, old copies and copies from Hong Kong circulate in the schools, and teachers actually prompt their pupils to read them without fear of persecution; the handful of artists and fiction-writers in Taipei deliberately avoid politics in their work; the historical art treasures Chiang Kai-shek removed from Peking in 1948 are on display as works of art, if indeed also as meriting national pride; and if you wish to listen to Beethoven or Wolf-Ferrari (banned as bourgeois by the Gang of Four) you may do so without regard to whether you are thereby helping the government's foreign policy of the day – the criterion for those composers' reinstatement in Peking.

A good deal has been reported abroad about the state of religion in China. For all Marxists, the words of Lenin must hold true: 'Any religious idea, any idea of any God at all, any flirtation even with a God, is the most inexpressible foulness.' In the past, the Chinese people have espoused three types of 'religious idea': there have been the imported world religions of Buddhism, Islam and Christianity; there have been the Confucian 'rites' of the family, practised at weddings and certain times of the year, which are sometimes connected with seasonal tillage of the soil and always symbolize the vitality of the lineage; and there has been an outworld of fortune-telling, shamanism and geomancy. Astride the three stands Taoism, providing rites in death, monastic retreats on Buddhist lines for the soul-weary living, and a home for fortune-tellers and shamans. Each of the types has its own holy writ – Bible, Qur'an and Sutras, Confucian classics, and for the last named the annual almanach which I found is still on sale everywhere outside China but is probably consulted less than when I was soaking up the Chinese way of life thirty years ago. The ecclesiastical dispute within the Catholic Church that resulted in proscription of the faith in China in 1717 concerned practice of Confucian rites by converts; even before the Liberation, only a minority of Chinese people followed one of the imported religions, but the greater number even of those few not only practised the 'rites' but, like the majority of their fellow countrymen, also took part in the third category: the biggest temple in Hong Kong, I noticed this time, has a flowery board outside that says, 'All gods can be worshipped here', and inside one which says, 'If you seek a boon, it is best to look reverent.'

After 1949, the Chinese Communist Party at first concerned itself only with the imported religions: Islam, not having strong ties abroad, was apparently not interfered with much; Christians were cut off from their strong overseas ties and made to submit to 'religious-work organs' under Party orders; and Buddhists were on one hand brought under similar 'organs', while on the other fresh links were sought by the Party, through pliant bonzes (Buddhist clerics), with Buddhist associations in foreign countries, as a means by which, in the absence of diplomatic recognition of the People's Republic, Chou Ên-lai could advance his foreign policy in the 1950s; it is supposed to have been Chou who chose the design for the new Buddha at the Ling Yin Monastery at Hangchow, original home of the Japanese Tendai sect.[2] Just as Party tolerance proved temporary in the economy, the arts, and every other aspect of life, so it was with religion, and the *People's Daily* admitted in June 1980 that 'during the turbulent decade, religious-work organs were abolished; their cadres and the faithful were maltreated and trampled underfoot; monasteries, temples and churches were closed and pulled down; religious relics were damaged and scriptures burned; and the people were prohibited from having any religious faith'. In the case of Buddhist bonzes, 'trampled underfoot' sometimes meant being beaten to death – even one or two of the pliant ones.

For myself, I saw only one church in China, and it had been adapted as a farm building; neither the Ling Yin Monastery nor the other Buddhist shrines I went to appeared to be an active place of worship, the handful of bonzes curators or mere caretakers dressed up, the Chinese crowds in them sightseers. At the Precious Lotus in Hong Kong or the Compass at Taipei, the majority of the crowd are sightseers too; but genuine worship also takes place, the monks are learned ordinands, and the lodgings are used as retreats. Although on the mainland individual freedom of belief is a constitutional right, organized freedom to ordain, teach and hold funds is not; and yet the *People's Daily* article just quoted admits both that there is popular discontent at the deprivation of the faithful and that the monasteries could be useful for foreign relations again. It looks as if the pre-Liberation policy has been reinstated, if not the bonzes; not many convinced Buddhists are likely to trust in the post-Mao tolerance, any more than writers and artists, and when Buddhist and Muslim 'religious-work organs' were permitted to meet again for the first time in Ch'ing-hai province (Tibet), to quote a single example, the only item on their agenda was the current Party line: believers' spiritual needs are as conspicuously absent from the policy as aesthetics from the Yenan Forum.

The irony is that, when it comes to the indigenous categories of worship, it is the peasants and working-class who keep up practices of the past condemned as repugnant to proletarian culture. During the Cultural Revolution, house-holds were called on to destroy the little altars found in every Chinese home for the Confucian rites; yet when one of Mr Frolic's refugees (Chapter 1) had a wedding in the house in the heyday of the Gang of Four, preliminaries and ceremony followed the traditional programme in every detail, the couple kowtowing to the ancestors at the spot where the altar used to be – all to the applause of the local Party secretary, slightly tipsy. As we noted before, the geomancers and shamans are back in evidence today, although I did not spot their locales. And so it is with the Overseas Chinese: growing enlightenment through education and a rising standard of living from the economic miracle have not abated the popular-ity of 'worship all gods here'; in the Hong Kong of 1979, although the Urban Council provides the actual cremation or burial for nothing, Taoist funerals are, so to speak, as lively as in the Peking of 1949, replete with crackers and gongs and paper houses and money to burn. All Chinese governments in this century – republican, communist and overseas – have curbed lavish spending on weddings and funerals as a social evil; I do not believe there has been any impact on the people's *inclination* in the matter.

Unlike the Japanese, the Chinese people seem to me never to have quite found their ideal blend of traditional and modern qualities of life. In Southeast Asia, the material standard of living is high, but the quality of life is less and less Chinese. Moreover, the political future is ominous: apart from political menaces outside their control among the host races of which Islamic socialism is one harbinger, the experience of the boat people causes not a few to look with anxiety on the growing military might and uncontrolled birthrate of a Marxist–Leninist Indochina and fear that one day there they may go themselves. Taiwan is still reasonably free and as Chinese as anybody likes or does not like, but the Chiang regime might not stand up to a world slump – even a slump in the Middle East. It could be argued that Hong Kong approaches nearest to the ideal – free, traditional, efficient, hygienic. It is true the Chinese peasant way of life has already succumbed there to an urbanization of unparalleled speed and intensity, and yet one sees among the tower blocks balconies of flower-pots and minute gardens, to the heart's content of a Shên Fu, contrived by the colonial architects for the tenants to tend, and, looking a little deeper, the gaudy signs of shamans and fortune-tellers who have moved in with them. At Wong Tai Sin Estate – the very name is of a Taoist 'immortal' – there has grown up *since 1973* a complex of 'worship halls' with little shops and stalls at the side for religious and fortune-telling 'software' that is a veritable superstition-market with a turnover of proportions unknown in less prosperous days.

Offering the palm of cold-war reconciliation, Chairman Hua in 1979 was inviting the people of Taiwan, Hong Kong and Macau to contribute their foreign skills to the Four Modernizations and make good from the capitalist miracle the generation lost under socialist transformation; British objections to 'red' trains on the Kowloon permanent way were dropped after thirty years, and Kowloon buses began to be built in China by Chinese labour managed by some Hong Kong capitalists, while other Hong Kong capitalists provided discreet hospitality for similar technical exchanges to be explored between Peking and Taipei. Hua's successors cannot extend the same invitation to other Overseas Chinese, of course, without fanning fears of Chinese imperialism in Southeast Asia. Taiwan, Hong Kong and Macau are due for eventual absorption into the mainland. Will it, in things of the spirit, be a recognizably Chinese mainland of *mellowed* Marxism, or must the peoples of those three places of refuge from

Liberation fall back in the end to Marxist proletarianization, in Manchester cloth caps and worker-suits? *If* the socialist miracle of economic transformation is ever wrought, perhaps the Chinese people will not notice.

Appendix: Old Tipsy's Look-out

'The district I have charge of is surrounded by mountains, with a range of sharp peaks to the southwest and lovely wooded ravines between them. The most verdant of the ravines has contrasting seams of cornelian running through its cliffs, and if you walk in among the foothills, after two or three miles you hear running water and come to a well where it gushes from the rocks. Where the path rounds a spur of the hill, there is a look-out high above. Nowadays it is called Old Tipsy's Look-out, for the mandarin comes here to tipple with his cronies, and after the fewest sips he is straightaway squiffy; being also a little on in years, he has the nickname Old Tipsy. He does not really come for the sake of the drink, but for the scenery – even if, as soon as he imbibes ever so little of that, his thoughts turn to the wine-pot as though he did.

'When the sun comes out the woodland mists disperse, and when the clouds gather again the grottoes fade from view – by this alternation of clear and hazy air morning and evening are distinguished on the mountains. Wild flowers bloom and fill the hollows with their scent; the fine old trees put forth their leaves and spread their umbrella of shade; then the winds blow up again, frost settles in, and the torrent dries up till its rocky bed is bare – by these signs the passing of the seasons is reckoned in the mountains. You can come out to the look-out any day of the year at dawn and return at dusk and still never tire of the variety of its scenery. You can watch the porters shouldering palankeens come jogging up the path, chanting in rhythm with their gait, and the travellers on foot who pause beneath the trees; you hear the calls of those behind and the answering shouts of the ones ahead. There is an endless throng of passers-by, backs bent beneath their burdens – all of them natives of these parts, busy about their daily errands. Anglers come to the spring to catch the fat fish in its deep pool, vintners to bottle its water and give their wine that extra "nose".

'The only banquet the mandarin has to offer his guests is game from the hills with humble spinach from the fields, cooked and served up quite without art. He hires no music of silken guitars or bamboo flutes to make it gay, but the cheers of the archers when they hit their bull's-eyes and the yells of the players who win at chess – the click of bamboo counters against horn beakers, and the mounting din of singing and jesting – these are what make the party go. And behold, in the middle of the revellers, that fellow with the silvering hair and the purple face has tumbled to the floor – the mandarin is dead-drunk!

'The reddening sun has set behind the mountains, and the blurred group of figures you cannot make out in the dusk is the mandarin tottering homewards, with his guests straggling behind. The trees of the forest have merged into one great shadow, and wild things begin to call to each other up and down the valley that the men are going away and birds and beasts can take joyful possession of the solitude. Yet the beasts and the birds know only the joys of mountain and forest – they know nothing of the pleasures of men. So too these men know the fun they had on their excursion with the mandarin, but they do not know the secret pleasure he gets from their fun: drunk, to take part in the merrymaking, but, sober again, to spin it all into a yarn is a private satisfaction of

Your obedient servant,
Ou-yang Hsiu of Lu Ling.'

Notes

NOTES TO CHAPTER ONE: PERCEPTIONS OF CHINESE LIFE

1. Richard W. Wilson *et al.* (eds), *Value Change in Chinese Society* (New York: Praeger, 1979).
2. Ross Terrill (ed.), *The China Difference* (New York: Harper & Row, 1979).
3. Desmond Neill, *Elegant Flower* (London: John Murray, 1956).
4. Probably the last such study in the field is C. Osgood's *The Chinese – a Hong Kong Community* (Tucson, 1975) 3 vols (which was first projected in 1938).
5. Austin Coates, *Myself a Mandarin – the Memoirs of a Special Magistrate* (London: Muller, 1968).
6. I had only just begun to learn Cantonese; but the use of an interpreter did not in itself distinguish me from the mandarins of old China, for, never natives of the district they were in charge of, they too spoke through local interpreters.
7. The English name of the country used by the Chinese Government in its foreign relations is 'People's Republic of China', but the Chinese name (influenced by euphony), *Chung-hua Jên-min Kung-ho-kuo*, is more literally 'Chinese People's Republic'. Sun Yat-sen's Republic of China, now confined to Taiwan, in Chinese *Chung-hua Min-kuo*, is similarly 'the Chinese Republic'. It will be noticed that the two governments use different words for 'republic': the communists say 'collective state', the nationalists 'citizen state'. Both words for 're public' occur in classical Chinese in other meanings and were first used in their modern sense in Japan.
8. Kang Chao, 'The China-Watchers Tested', *The China Quarterly*, no. 81 (March 1980).
9. *Washington Post*, 11 April 1980.
10. B. M. Frolic, *Mao's People* (Cambridge, Mass.: Harvard University Press, 1980).
11. Simon Leys, *Chinese Shadows* (Harmondsworth: Penguin, 1978).

NOTES TO CHAPTER TWO: SOCIALIST TRANSFORMATION AND
ECONOMIC MIRACLE

1. R. J. Lifton, *Revolutionary Immortality* (London: Weidenfeld & Nicolson, 1969).

2. Dyer Ball, *Things Chinese* (Shanghai, 1903).
3. *Value Change in Chinese Society.*

NOTES TO CHAPTER THREE: TOILERS OF THE FAR EAST

1. 'Gratis' in the People's Republic means in exchange for commendation as models to be emulated by fellow-workers – as model scabs, critics might sneer.
2. Shên Fu, *Fou-shêng liu chi* ('Six Chapters of an Aimless Life'), part 2: *Hsien ch'ing chi ch'ü* ('Recollections in Tranquillity').
3. There was formerly some confusion to the ear in the fact that *kung-hui* for 'trade union' sounded exactly the same, in all Chinese dialects, as *kung-hui* for 'guild', although the two *kungs* are written with totally different characters; *kung-shê* for 'commune' uses the *kung* of 'guild', *kung-ch'an* for 'communist' a third *kung* pronounced in a different tone.
4. Leong Choon Cheong, *Youth in the Army* (Singapore: Federal Publications, 1978).

NOTES TO CHAPTER FOUR: BOILING SMALL FISH

1. The National People's Congress convened at Peking in 1980 and, among other radical changes, *announced* a policy of individual taxation for the future, applicable at first only to the upper élite.

NOTES TO CHAPTER FIVE: FROM MANDARIN TO CADRE

1. *On the Party* (1954) and *How to Be a Good Communist* (1939).
2. See especially the history of 'Ten Mile Inn' given by Isabel and David Crook, *Mass Movement in a Chinese Village* (London: Routledge & Kegan Paul, 1979).
3. Lucian W. Pye, *The Spirit of Chinese Politics: a Psychocultural Study of the Crisis in Political Development* (Cambridge, Mass.: M.I.T. Press, 1968).
4. See Robert J. Lifton, *Thought Reform and the Psychology of Totalism – a Study of 'Brainwashing' in China* (London: Gollancz, 1961), especially part 2: 'Thought Reform of Chinese Intellectuals'.
5. An anthology of the explanations put before the Chinese people and the rest of the world in the name of the Chinese Party's Central Committee was published in Peking in 1965, to celebrate the downfall of Khrushchev, as *The Polemic on the General Line of the International Communist Movement*.
6. The Chinese word for 'proletariat' (*wu-ch'an chieh-chi*) does not refer to breeding of more labourers but means 'the class without resources'.
7. Examples of both malpractices are contained in B. M. Frolic's book, *Mao's People.*

NOTES TO CHAPTER SIX: THE CHINESE INTELLECTUAL CRISIS

1. The word 'Maoism' is inappropriate and not used in China. Only the Four Sages of Communism (Marx, Engels, Lenin and Stalin) are revered as exponents of an '-ism': Mao laid claim only to a lesser degree of originality by adopting 'thought'.
2. See H. H. Welch, *Buddhism under Mao* (Cambridge, Mass.: Harvard University Press, 1972) especially pp. 187ff.

Index